MW01658472

DEEP THOUGHTS FOR YOUNG THINKERS

ANSWERS TO QUESTIONS ABOUT GOD, THE BIBLE, AND LIFE

JOHN DANIEL McWILLIAMS

Deep Thoughts for Young Thinkers:
Answers to Questions About God, the Bible, and Life

Copyright© 2021 by John D. McWilliams.
All rights reserved. No part of this work may be reproduced, stored, or transmitted in any form or by any means—electronic, mechanical, digital, photocopy, audio recording—except for brief quotations in printed reviews, without prior permission from the author.

Published by Rose Rock Media.
Visit www.ThinkingAboutTheBible.com for more resources and information.

ISBN- 978-1-7333997-3-9

Scripture passages within the text are paraphrases by the author. The Scripture list at the end of the book is from The ESV® Bible (The Holy Bible, English Standard Version®), copyright © 2001 by Crossway, a publishing ministry of Good News Publishers. Used by permission. All rights reserved. Every effort was made to present this material accurately and honestly. This material is the opinion of the author and is intended only to encourage discussion. The author will not be held responsible for its misuse or any conceivable harmful use.

P1022A1

Assistant Editor – Bonnie McWilliams

Special thanks to Grace Morrison, Jordan Sonsel, and Connie Goodson for their encouragement and expertise with young people.

Contents

Should I *think* about spiritual things?

This may seem to be a strange question, but there are those who say Christians should rely on *feeling* rather than *knowing*—that this makes us more spiritual.

Suppose you want to make a new friend. So, you select a suitable person and start studying them. Every day you watch the person. You ask people around you about the person. You find out about them online. Eventually, you know all about them. You know their favorite music, what they watch on TV, their hobbies—you know them *very well*.

Not only would this be creepy, it would be a lousy way to build a friendship. In fact, would that person even be your friend? Does knowing *about* someone make it a relationship? Of course not! Friendship is about being *with* someone—knowing about them personally and enjoying their presence. Talking with them. Laughing. Crying. Going places with them. Doing things together.

But consider this… When you have a friendship, don't you also *know* things about the person? At first you knew a little about them (that's why you became interested in them). Then by being with your friend, you learn more and more about them. The more time you spend with them the more you know them. You know their habits, their favorites, their fears. After a while you even finish each other's sentences. By having a *feeling* relationship, you also develop a *knowing* relationship. *Both are important!*

Unlike other religions, Christianity is about a *relationship* with your Creator, not just knowing about Him and learning a bunch of rules! Jesus came into the world so that we could *know* him—not just study him. However, just as with our other friends, we learn more about Him as the relationship grows.

It's easy for some people to go to one extreme or the other in their relationship with God. You probably wouldn't like it if one day your best friend said, "I don't want to know anything else about you. I just want to enjoy the friendship we have now." A real friend would *want* to know more and more about you. Friendships are constantly growing. In the same way, as our relationship with Jesus grows, we should want to *know* Him better.

In His Word, the Bible, God has given us many details about what He is like. Since He is our friend, He wants us to know Him. The more we know about him, the stronger our relationship with Him grows. Over the years, our organized learning about God has become known as *theology*. The facts God has revealed about Himself and His creation are called *doctrines*.

Often when someone uses the words *theology* or *doctrine*, the reaction is, "Oh, no… more boring, brainy stuff!" In a way, that's sort of true. Studying the facts without considering the relationship can be boring. And sadly, there are many people who spend their whole life learning about God, yet they never have a relationship with him. But can you imagine learning facts about your best-friend-forever who happens to be the Creator of the universe and *you*? Could anything be more exciting!

So, should Christians think? Yes! Jesus said you should "love the Lord your God with all your heart and with all your soul and *with all your mind*."[1] He wants

[1] Matthew 22:37

you to *think* about Him and *learn* about Him so that you can *love* Him more and more!

We'll look at theology and doctrines often in this book but always remember, our purpose in knowing *about* God is to grow our friendship *with* God.

Is it all okay to use logic and reason in studying God and the Bible?

God values faith, but He gives abundant evidence of His truths. Over the centuries, very intelligent Christians have uncovered strong, real-world indications of God and what the Bible teaches. Unlike other religions, the Christian's faith is reasonable and based in reality. It has stood firmly through over two thousand years of doubt, ridicule, and criticism. We would expect nothing less of an Almighty Creator!

The organized study of the evidence for Christian truth is called *apologetics*. ("Apologize" literally means to *give a reason*, not to *be sorry*.) In the next sections, we'll use a lot of apologetics.

ABOUT GOD…

How do I find out about God?

I've never met George Washington. He must have been an interesting person. His home, Mount Vernon, still stands in Virginia. Even though no one living today was a personal friend of Washington, we can know a lot about him by visiting his house. We can see what his mealtime would have been like. We can imagine that he was an organized person by the design of the farm. We can see by the architecture and furnishings that he enjoyed simple beauty and practicality.

The Bible tells us that we can know a little bit about God from observing what He has made. Our earth (in fact, the whole universe) is an orderly place, filled with beauty. Atoms and molecules behave in specific ways. Animals and plants seem to live in purposeful relationships with each other. Planets, stars, and galaxies move in orderly, predictable patterns. Moreover, we have sensory organs and brains that can actually perceive all of this!

The Creation (universe) seems to be here and do things "on purpose" and not just randomly. Even people who have never read God's Word believe there is something (someone) out there who started everything. We might even go a step farther and say that this "someone" must be orderly and creative. He must enjoy beauty. He must care for us since He made us capable of observing and appreciating His creation. These "clues" about our Creator are a type of *general knowing*.[2]

Washington's home gives a small peek at what he was like. His writings, however, tell us much more about him. When I read what Washington wrote, I know him much more personally. As powerfully as nature speaks to us about the Creator, God wanted us to know even more about him. Unfortunately, our limited human minds alone could never come close to learning more about the unlimited Creator of everything. Unless He decided to *tell* us more, we would never be able to know more.

Thankfully, God was willing to tell us about himself! In His written Word, the Bible, God gave us everything He wanted us to know about Him personally. The Bible is a type of *special knowing*. It tells us some of the things about God that we could never have learned any other way. Parts of Scripture are stories of how God dealt with other people. We learn a lot about God's character by the way He interacted with Noah, Abraham, Moses, David, and many others. The events in the *Old Testament* (the first part of the Bible, written before Jesus came to earth) let us know that God is trustworthy, all-knowing, all-powerful, wise, and loving. He also spoke through special messengers (prophets) about His nature and what pleases him.

In the *New Testament* (the second part of the Bible) God spoke to us in a very unexpected way. The Creator of the universe actually came to earth Himself as the

---

[2] Or *general revelation*...facts about God revealed by nature. God's Word is considered *special revelation*.

man Jesus. For the first time, people could communicate with God face-to-face! Jesus even said that whoever saw Him was seeing God.[3] In human form, Jesus showed us many things about God through His teaching and His actions.

Today, we have the benefit of the Old and New Testaments to give us information about God. Through the Bible, God gives us every single fact that we need to know Him and enjoy living in His creation. But simply having the Scriptures doesn't mean we know what they say. The Bible encourages us to study it and keep on learning about God and reality. I know many very old people who say they have studied God's Word all their lives and are still finding new and amazing things about him.

It's also important to listen to God's teachers. He often explains the Bible to me through other Christians such as pastors, teachers, and even my friends. God also promised to send His Spirit to help us understand the truths He has given through the Bible. The most important thing is to stay close to your Creator Friend who loves you and wants you to know him! We stay closest to Him when we read of Him in the Bible. Then we pray, think about him, and listen as the Spirit makes things clear.

[3] John 14:9

What is God like?

So, if God has given us all the facts He wants us to know about him, just what *do* we know about him?

For sure, I can never know all there is to know about God. My tiny three-pound brain could never contain the unlimited Creator of everything! I'm sure I'll learn more about Him in eternity with Him someday—face-to-face. But for now, I can trust Him and be satisfied with what His Word tells me.

Yet from a human perspective we know many things about God through His *revelation* or revealing of himself. We call God's characteristics His *attributes*. As mentioned earlier, the organized study of God is called theology. Organization makes understanding things a lot easier, so let's do a little theology. I'll list several attributes that God has revealed about Himself in the Bible. Let's also use the same fancy words that *theologians* (studiers of God) use. Try to learn them if you can, since these are good ways to describe and share God's attributes to others…

Self-existing – This doesn't mean He made Himself exist, but that His existence depends only on Himself. God never *began* to exist because He has always existed. There was never a time when God didn't exist. There will never be a time when He doesn't exist… Understand? Of course not! We limited creatures can never understand completely how that works. We'll look at this again later (Hebrews 13:8).

Omnipotent – It's a big word that simply means "all-powerful." There is no limit to God's power in any way. Anything that can be done, God can do it (Jeremiah 32:17).

Omniscient – Another big word that means "all-knowing." There is nothing that God doesn't know. From the smallest detail to every thought in every person's head, God knows it. He also knows every past event as well as every future event. Nothing can be hidden from God (Isaiah 46:9-10).

Omnipresent – This means that God is everywhere. He doesn't have to *go* anywhere because He is already there. There isn't a place in the universe (or outside the universe) where God is not. This doesn't mean He can't come in special ways, such as when He came to Moses on Mt. Sinai (Psalm 139:7-12).

Personal – God is a person—not just a "force" (like on *Star Wars*). He has a personality in the same ways that you do. God thinks, feels, loves, laughs, and wills. (Exodus 3:14)

Holy – God is completely different and separate from everything that He has made. We can try to compare Him with other things as learning tools, but there is no real way to compare God with anything else (1 Samuel 2:2).

Triune – In a way we cannot comprehend, God is three Persons yet one God. He has revealed Himself as Father,

Son, and Spirit. We'll discuss this more later (Philippians 1:2, Titus 2:13, Acts 5:3–4).

Immutable – God never changes—not even in the tiniest way. Being perfect there is no need to change (Malachi 3:6).

Sovereign – This means that God acts because of His own decisions. No one or no thing forces Him to do anything (Daniel 4:35).

Loving – God is perfectly devoted to the well-being of others (1 John 4:7-8).

Righteous – There is nothing evil, wrong, or imperfect in God (Psalm 71:19).

Just – God is completely fair in everything He does (Deuteronomy 32:4).

Good – God is absolute goodness within himself, and His acts express goodness to other beings (Psalm 34:8).

Merciful – God often decides to *not* give us the bad consequences of our sin (1 Peter 1:3).

Graceful – God often decides to give us good things even though we don't deserve them (Exodus 34:6).

We can "kind of" understand some of these truths about God, but many of them still stump us. That's why He had to *reveal* them to us, since our imperfect, limited minds have problems grasping ideas that are perfect or unlimited. To explain them to us would be like teaching a difficult math problem to a one-year-old. For now, we trust God's love, mercy, and goodness and accept His more difficult characteristics. (In heaven, I believe we will begin to understand even these difficult ideas.)

Where did God come from?

This question definitely shows how limited our understanding can be. God didn't come from anywhere because He has always been! He is *eternal*.

We have difficulty comprehending something that has always existed since everything we observe around us was caused by something else. This is called the principle of *cause and effect*. You push a swing (cause) and it moves (effect). Your parents (cause) had a child (effect).

Let's apply a little logical thinking. Try to go backward along the cause-and-effect chain…

What allowed you to push the swing? Your muscles.

What allowed your muscles to move? The bowl of cereal you had for breakfast.

What caused the grain to have energy? The sun.

What caused the sun to shine… and so on and so on…

But do you see that we can't keep going back forever? It also doesn't make sense that something could just pop into existence out of nothing. At this point, we have to imagine the very first "cause" that started everything. The ancient Greek thinkers considered this the *First Cause*—something that had to have always been, that had nothing that caused it. Christians believe that God was the First Cause.

This seems quite believable since God claims to be the first cause. Also, it would make sense that the first cause would have to be greater in all ways than the effects it creates. Something can't produce another thing more complex than itself.

As God on earth, Jesus claimed to be eternal. He called Himself the "Alpha and Omega, the Beginning and the End" (the first and last letters of the Greek alphabet). This didn't mean that He had a beginning or an end, but in a way our minds could understand He was saying that He exists throughout eternity, from past to future.

God has also created us as eternal beings. Although we all had a beginning, we are promised that we won't have an end. We are said to be *everlasting*. Certainly, my body will someday end, but my spirit, the real me, will live forever. Those who trust in Jesus will enjoy eternal (everlasting) life with Him in heaven forever and ever. At that time, maybe we'll begin to understand eternity!

Does God have a name other than "God?"

In our culture parents choose their children's names for a variety of reasons. Sometimes the name is from a relative. Sometimes it's just because the parents like it. In the cultures described in the Bible, it was common to name someone according to what parents expected a child to be like. A person might even receive a name later in life. This name would be a description of what the person did or what they were like.

The English word "god" simply refers to any imagined supreme being. We capitalize it as "God" when speaking of the God of the Bible (the true supreme being). When the God of the Bible told Moses His "personal" name, it obviously wasn't just a pretty name or one that was given to him. The Creator of the universe identified Himself with a term that best revealed His nature. Translated into English, God told Moses that His name was "I Am" (or more like "I Am Because I Am").[4] What an appropriate name for God! In this special name, God declares His attributes of self-existence, eternity, and holiness. He simply *is* with no need for anything else.

In Moses's language, this name was pronounced something like *Yahweh* (Yah-Way). We're not completely sure about the pronunciation since the Hebrew language doesn't use written vowels. Also, early Hebrews wouldn't say this name of God out loud because they considered it too holy and special. They simply wrote the name with its consonants: YHWH.

When they spoke of God, they would often use other names for Him such as *Adonai* ("my Lord") or *Elohim* ("the God"). The word "Yahweh" was produced by inserting the vowels from Adonai and Elohim into the YHWH consonants. As the name was translated into

---

[4] Exodus 3:14

Latin and eventually English it became the word "Jehovah."

Since biblical names define a person, God has many other names and titles to express the many ways He interacts with us. For example, the Bibles calls Him (in English translation)…

Yahweh Who Heals
Yahweh the Provider
Yahweh My Shepherd
God Almighty
Lord of Hosts
The Most High

Digging Deeper In most English-language Bibles, the word "Lord" is often used when a name for God is written. When you see the word printed in small caps (LORD), it indicates "Jehovah." If printed normally (Lord), it's "Adonai." The Jewish people were correct in honoring the special name of God. One of the Ten Commandments says to keep the name of God special and not use it frivolously or without a good reason. Too often today, we hear God's name used wrongly such as "Oh my God!" or even worse. How it must disappoint God to hear His name said so often yet honored so little.

Is the Christian's God the same as Allah, Buddha, Brahman, and others?

Some religious people claim that all the gods of the different religions are just different ways of thinking about the same being. They often say that as long as one sincerely worships *a god*, it doesn't matter which one. Many with good intentions of tolerance and inclusion tell us we should consider all religions' deities equal and acceptable.

In one sense, the name we call God doesn't matter. Some people may use the Hebrew name *Yahweh* while others pronounce it *Jehovah* or call Him *Lord* or *God*. The Greek name for God is *Theos*, the root used in several languages such as the Spanish *Dios*. These are all referring to the same being—the God of the Bible.

However, it's a different matter altogether when a name for God refers to a different being with a totally different history, relationship, and communication. For example, when a Muslim speaks of the supreme being he worships, is his *Allah* just another name for Yahweh? Some would say yes, since they are both thought of as the supreme spiritual being who interact with humans.

But the Muslim's Allah is defined in a completely different context compared with the God of the Bible. The Islamic belief denies that Allah is a trinity. There is no Son, therefore, no cross, resurrection, or payment for our sin. Islam demands that a person earn their way to "heaven" by giving service to Allah.

Hindu and Buddhist "gods" are mere "forces" and not personal. Their ideas of sin and redemption are nothing like biblical truths. Like every other human-made religion, they require people *do* things for salvation rather than accept what has already been *done*.

Today, it's common to hear sweet-sounding memes like "All roads lead to God." This is far from the truth found in the Bible. Yahweh God says "I am the Lord. There is no other!"[5] Moreover, Jesus claimed there is only *one* to God, and He assured us that He *is* the only way to know Him.

Why does God let bad things happen?

It's no secret that bad things happen all the time. What was the last bad thing that happened to you?

Some bad things are not too bad… I dropped my phone in the puddle… There's a pimple on my nose…

Some are really bad… a severe illness… the death of someone you love…

Many people ponder this problem. Some people get mad at God when bad things occur. They ask "If God is all-powerful, *couldn't* He have stopped this tragedy? If God is loving *wouldn't* He stop this tragedy?"

These are good questions that sometimes cause people to turn away from God or doubt that He is what He claims to be. In fact, many who are opposed to God and Christianity say that some "tragic event" in their life was the cause. What answers can we give someone in this situation?

---

[5] Isaiah 45:5

When we have a problem with God or the Bible, it's usually a good idea to consider whether the problem might be in our *thinking* rather than with God or His Word. Sometimes it's wise to back up and see the "big-picture" of life and reality rather than focus on the problem. Let's look at some ways Scripture deals with bad things…

First of all, it's important to see that God didn't intend for bad things to be a part of His creation. In the very first chapter of the Bible, God looks at His creation and says, "It is good!" It wasn't until the sin and rebellion of humans that this world started falling apart and things began to go wrong. We'll discuss this event later, but for now just note that God created "good" and people brought about "bad."

Then can't God fix this problem? The answer is a definite "Yes!" The entire story throughout Scripture is about Jesus coming to earth and sacrificing Himself to reset the world back to "good." This is called *redemption*. Jesus died to *redeem* not just the things of the world, but the people of the world! God was able and willing to deal with the "badness" caused by human sin. Yet that brings up another issue—timing.

After thousands of years of "badness," God is still in the process of making things right again, but we're very impatient creatures. We want our problems fixed now. That's okay. Sometimes God does fix our problems quickly. He may immediately heal disease, supply needs, and mend relationships—or He may wait. We're promised that in the future, Jesus will return to earth and completely eliminate sin, evil, and all bad things. The world will be just like heaven is now—

perfect and good, without pain, suffering, or unhappiness.

Another thing to consider is that very often, bad things can bring about good things. You've likely heard "No pain, no gain." We see this in many ways. An athlete suffers through hours of agony to reach a physical goal. A mother endures the pain of childbirth in order to enjoy the love of a child. Imagine trying to explain to a four-year-old why Mommy and Daddy want to put her in a hospital so that a medicine can make her sick then cause her to be weak, miserable, and bald. Yet the parents know that it's the only way to stop the cancer that's hurting their child. From God's view, bad things can bring good things. From our view—it hurts!

Scripture tells us that not everything that comes our way will be good, but it can definitely work to bring about good.[6] Unfortunately, we don't always know immediately what God is up to in our lives. This is when we must trust in His attributes of love, mercy, grace, wisdom, and omniscience. We know that whatever God allows in our lives is best for us because He is perfectly *good.* Like a good parent He is more concerned with our long-term well-being than our momentary suffering.

Sometimes, I get either too busy or too selfish to keep a strong friendship with God. God knows that I am happiest when I trust Him and rest in His love and friendship. Even when I stray from him, God still loves me. He might use problems and suffering to cause me to see my condition and want to come back to him.

Even though we know things will turn out good in the end, it's still not pleasant to have to deal with

---

[6] Romans 8:28

troubles and sorrows from day to day. The Apostle Paul encourages us to try and keep that big-picture view of things mentioned earlier. He says that our "brief" problems here on earth will seem worth it some day when we look back from an eternal perspective.[7] Compared with our future everlasting joy, our present pain and sorrows will seem very small!

Are there things God can't do?

Sometimes people say that God can do *anything*. He is, after all, omnipotent. We also describe Him as unlimited, unbounded, absolute, and perfect. But are there things that God simply can't do?

You may have heard the riddle: *Can God create a stone so big that He can't lift it?* The question shows faulty thinking about God and His nature. God can't do something that can't be done. This may sound like silliness, but it's really only a language problem. The stone-lifting question is an example of a *logical impossibility*. In other words, it isn't logically possible for "A" to be "not A", or for 1 + 1 to not equal 2. In simplistic terms, logical impossibilities and absurdities don't exist in reality, so whether God can "do" them is a non-question. This doesn't mean that God is limited by logic and mathematics. These concepts are part of God's eternal nature—absurd ideas are not.

---

[7] 2 Corinthians 4:17

Being total perfection, any one of God's attributes can't contradict another attribute. For example, some ask why He can't simply ignore our sins just because He wants to? It's because that application of His *mercy* would contradict His attribute of *justness* (fairness).

God is also *holy* which means he's "set apart" or "different" from all His creation. This requires that He *not* be some things. God can't be the same as something He created, so there are many things His nature forbids Him from being.

Scripture gives several other truths about God's limitations. Hebrews 6:18 tells us that it's "impossible for God to lie." For Him to be untruthful would be in opposition to His character. Scripture also tells us that God can't change, be unfaithful, act unjustly, and anything else contrary to His nature.

Is God just the "feeling of love" among people?

John 4:16 tells us "God is love, and whoever stays in love stays in God." This verse is often quoted by those who think of God as a "force" rather than a real being. They like to think of our Creator as a worldwide "feeling of happiness" that doesn't hold us accountable for sin.

It's clear from other scriptures that God is so much more than this. He also has attributes such as righteousness, holiness, goodness, justice, and many others. Moreover, God is a *person* with consciousness, emotions, and will. When John referred to God as "love"

He was emphasizing one of the Creator's most important attributes for Christians. Because God perfectly displays the attribute of love, He redeemed us from our sin and gave us eternal life!

The attribute of love does make God different from other supposed gods of other religions. Other gods are claimed to be loving, but it is more of an "add-on" to their personality. The God of the Bible has had love within His very being from all eternity. But who did He love before creating other beings? Only a *triune* God can solve this paradox. The three Persons of the Trinity have been in an eternal loving relationship. Love has always existed and is the driving force of God's dealings with us, yet it is only one of his perfect attributes.

Did humans invent the idea of God just to meet their needs?

Some unbelievers claim that humans made up gods and other "superheroes" because they feared death, or they wanted to explain complicated things. They would say the God of the Bible is just wishful thinking.

It's true that many people groups who have never heard of the Bible make up imaginary gods and goddesses to explain the world around them. Maybe we should turn the question around and ask why people seem to have a deep-down urge to make up gods.

Someone once said that we seem to have a "God-shaped" space in our hearts that only God can fill.[8] Perhaps it makes more sense to say that since God made us specifically to have a relationship with Him that He also put that aspect inside us. We have a *need* for a "god" because that's how the true God designed us! We desire happiness because we were designed to live in a happy place. We don't like it when things go wrong because we were designed for a place where things don't go wrong.

Of course, this reasoning only gives an alternative view. In other sections, we'll look at specific evidence for the true God.

How can one God be three persons?

When Jesus came to earth, many people began asking this same question. Throughout the Old Testament, God's people were one of the few groups to worship *only* one God This is called *monotheism*. Other people groups believed in *polytheism* which says there are many gods. This was an extremely important truth, and God reminded His people many times that He was the *only true God.*

Then, Jesus was born…

Jesus claimed to be God. When some people realized what He was saying, they were angered. "There is only one God! And He is in heaven! And He is not a

[8] Blaise Pascal

man!" Many wanted to kill Jesus for making this claim. Others just assumed He was crazy or a liar.

Sometimes God reveals things about Himself slowly over a period of time. He often does that for us, too. It probably wouldn't work very well if math teachers decided to teach first graders everything there was to know about math. Just stuff those little heads full of fractions, and long division, and algebra all at once!

Many things that were *concealed* in the Old Testament are *revealed* in the New Testament. Even Jesus's disciple had trouble understanding how Jesus could be God as a man here on earth and still be in heaven running things. Jesus even prayed to God His Father who was in heaven. How does that work!

This was one of the first clues to a very important attribute of *God*. Jesus called Himself God's *son,* but He also claimed to be *the* only God. So, there are two Gods? One God (the father one) made another God (the son)? No.

This is where it gets interesting. But while you're puzzling, let's add another piece of the puzzle. There's a third God, in addition to the Father and Son. Jesus said there's a Spirit of God who is neither the Father nor the Son. So, three Gods? Yes and no…

A lot of people have spent a lot of time thinking about all of this. Some have tried to explain it by saying it's like a girl could be a daughter, a niece, and a sister all at the same time. But it's not really like that. Some have said it's like H_2O can be water, ice, or steam. But it's not really like that either. In fact, it's not like anything else!

Remember, one of God's attributes is holiness. That means He's *totally* different from anything else. I can try as hard as I might, but my limited little brain won't be able to understand how this works, yet it's one of the clearest ideas taught in Scripture. God is a *triune* God, unlike any other being. His three *persons*, the Father, Son, and Holy Spirit are one single God just as the Old Testament people believed.

We call these three persons the *Trinity*. We say the Trinity is "one God in three persons." (And no, it's not like three kings sharing a throne or conjoined triplets.) Since God has always existed and can't change in any way, that means the Trinity has always existed. Even before the creation of the universe, the three Persons of the Trinity loved and communicated with each other.

At a point in our history, God the Father sent His son (often called the 2nd Person of the Trinity) to be born into a human body (Jesus). The Holy Spirit (3rd Person of the Trinity) was also active on the earth and continues to work today. Even though He is usually working in the "background," the Holy Spirit is just as much God as the other two persons.[9]

Confused? That's quite alright. Remember, many things about God are difficult for our limited minds to grasp. While we look forward to a time in eternity when we see Him more clearly, we can rest now in the fact that God understands it all, and that He understands our lack of understanding.

---

[9] In Luke 3:22, all three persons are present at the baptism of Jesus. See if you can find them.

Why doesn't God come down and prove himself?

If God really wants people to believe in him, why doesn't He come down from heaven and let us see him? Wouldn't a few simple miracles here and there fill the churches?

That's a very good question, since God obviously has the power to do that. We also know that He really wants to have a personal relationship with each one of us. Since God is all-wise and all-knowing, there must be a good reason for His "hiddenness." There are several reasons that might explain this.

One day when I was very young, my dad said he was taking me to a fishing spot he found when he was a boy. We set out through a thick forest on a path I had never used before. It was a scary place and at that point, I could have questioned my dad's plan. I could have said, "Wait, Dad… Can you show me a map to make sure you know where you're going? Or can you explain where this place is?"

But I knew my dad and I knew he loved me. He had always been honest, intelligent, and wise. My relationship with him allowed me to have *faith* in His love, ability, and intentions. I really didn't need the *sight* of a map! I'm sure my dad was more pleased that I trusted him than if I had demanded a detailed plan.

God places importance on our *faith* in Him. He is pleased when we "…walk by *faith*, not by *sight*."[10] God

[10] 2 Corinthians 5:7

desires the kind of relationship with us that leads us to trust His plans. This doesn't mean He's angry when we look for evidence of Him. When the apostle Thomas doubted that Jesus had risen from the dead in a physical body, Jesus came to him and asked him to examine His wounds to see if He was real. I'm glad we have Thomas's example, because I sometimes need a little more proof as well. God is kind enough to give evidence when we sincerely need it.

Also, when we take the first step of putting faith in God's intentions, He often gives us bits of evidence that prove our faith was correct. However, the usual order is *faith* first, *seeing* second.

But back to the question… "Why doesn't God come down and show himself?"

Actually, He already has in a very real sense! God literally came to earth as the man Jesus. The Creator God walked among humans as another human. He performed miracles that only God could do. Sadly, even this didn't convince most people, and even today most people don't believe the truth of these historical events.

Also, the first chapter of Romans tells us that God is certainly making Himself known…

> Through the created universe, we can clearly see the invisible God and His true nature and power (Romans 1:20).

We live in a purposeful world that couldn't have "just happened." Our universe is orderly, complex, and beautiful, telling us that there must be a Creator who values those things, and has the power to bring them about.

Is it arrogant for God to want to be praised and worshipped?

Suppose a friend of yours devotes her whole life to medical research. One day, she discovers and new medicine that can cure every disease known to man? Your friend is so generous, she decides to make the medicine available to everyone on earth absolutely free! Not only that, she uses all her money to travel the world making sure everyone gets the medicine.

"What a great person!" everyone says. And that would be very true. She obviously is one of the most noble people to ever lived. But suppose the people of the world got together and held a special ceremony to honor this very noble person. Then suppose she was given a golden trophy and asked to say a few words…

She takes the microphone and says "Yes, I am indeed a great person! I'm selfless, humble, and definitely the greatest person who has ever lived! I so deserve this great honor!"

I'm guessing a silence would move over the audience. The people would look puzzled and start whispering among themselves.

We seem to know deep inside that no one is really perfect, no matter how much we appreciate or admire them. It's okay to get praise from others for a job well done, but for someone to sing their own praises—that's different. A humble spirit is a good companion for greatness.

Some people are bothered by the fact that God tells us in His Word that we should *praise*, *worship*, and *glorify* Him. Is this something that a good God would do?

Once again, our human perspective might be clouding reality. Remember, one of God's attributes is *holiness*. He really is completely different from everything else. God alone is the only perfect thing (person) in the universe.

As an earthly father, if I wanted my children to be ultimately happy, I would want to give them the most perfect, valuable gift I could. Since a relationship with God truly is the one thing that will make His child happy, why would He wish for us less than the best? By encouraging us to see and admire His true nature, He is actually giving us the thing that will ultimately give us the most joy!

Some are also disturbed by the fact that God said at times He is *jealous*. God's jealousy wants His children to be true to Him and not to follow idols or false gods. In the same way, God's jealousy is good since He knows that idols and false gods can never bring His children true joy.

Praising and worshipping God isn't like praising and worshipping any other person or thing since a relationship with Him is what we were made for. Nothing else can bring us ultimate joy. God is *good to us* by wanting our worship to focus on Him!

ABOUT BECOMING A CHRISTIAN…

What is sin?

Most of us know the answer to this question without much instruction, but let's look at it biblically…

The Bible speaks of sin as "missing the mark." Imagine an archer aiming for the center of a target. When an arrow hits somewhere off-center, the mark has been missed.

God is perfect and He created a perfect universe. Everything was "right on the mark." Nothing was off-center. But when other beings with wills of their own were created, marks were missed. Anything that isn't "on-target" with God's perfect will is sin…

What's so bad about sin?

Did you ever notice that when a strong odor is nearby, it seems to go away after a while? After several minutes of sensing a smell, our noses become *desensitized* to that odor. We stop smelling it even though it's still there.

We can easily become desensitized to sin. At first a certain sin (ours or someone else's) may seem awful. After a while, though, if we're constantly exposed to that same sin, it begins to lose its "awfulness."

Even the most godly humans sin regularly and are always around people who sin. We get so used to sin that it doesn't seem as bad as it really is. And unfortunately, as the world gets more and more sinful, we tend to get more and more desensitized to it.

God, however, is perfectly holy and good. He sees sin as what it really is. His standards never change even though our attitudes might. God desires that the universe be perfect and righteous, just as He is. Any imperfection in it (sin), makes it a place that is *less good* for the creatures He made to live in it. Just as a parent might hate the germs that are making their child feel sick, God hates the sin that makes humans miserable. He will do whatever it takes to eliminate it. (Which happened to be the death of His Son!)

Scripture encourages us to have God's view of sin, no matter what society tells us. By seeing sin for what it is and opposing it, we make the world more glorifying to God and a better place for His creatures.

Are some sins worse than others?

Suppose a passing car flips a small pebble through a store's big glass window and cracks it. Now suppose a car goes out of control and runs through another window. Which window is broken? Both…

The Bible warns against different sins such as lying, stealing, lust, pride, murder, cheating, and many others. When we see lists of sins, we often think some are *big sins* and some are *small sins*. Obviously, some sins have bigger consequences than others. Murder is much worse than cheating on a test—right?

Yes, the consequences are greater, and from our view more harm is done by murder. Even our court system supports this idea. But according to our original definition, both sins "miss the mark" of God's perfection. (Both result in a "broken window.")

In one sense, God is more concerned with the *attitude* that caused the sin than the sin itself. Jesus said that if someone hates another person so much that they want to kill them, they have already committed murder in their heart. The *decision* to commit a sin is when the mark is actually missed—before the sin is *done*. I'm saddened when I think of the sins I've committed in my mind. Even though I never had the opportunity to *do* the sin, I am still guilty.

Seem hopeless? How can we ever live up to God's high standard? *That's why it's called "good news!"* Jesus died to 1) forgive my sins, and 2) to give His Spirit to renew my mind and help me *not* to sin…

> If we confess our sins, God will be faithful and just to forgive us and to remove all unrighteousness from us (1 John 1:9).

What exactly is salvation?

Sometimes the words we use about Christians beliefs are confusing to those who are unfamiliar with the Bible or church. Very often, even believers hear "church-phrases" that we may not completely understand.

"Salvation" or "being saved" is likely the most important idea in Scripture, but its meaning often slips by. It's the reason Jesus came to earth and died, so God's Word has much to say about people being *saved*…

> Everyone who calls on the name of the Lord will be **saved.** (Romans 10:13)
>
> By grace you have been **saved** through your faith. And even this is not your own doing. It is the gift of God (Ephesians 2:8).
>
> Believe in the Lord Jesus, and you will be **saved** (Acts 16:31).
>
> God **saved** us and called us to be holy, not because of our works but because of His own purpose and grace, which He gave us in Christ Jesus (2 Timothy 1:9)

But just what do we need to be saved *from*? From what threat did Jesus rescue us? The simple answer is that we must be saved from *sin and its consequence that a holy God must apply*… Scripture tells us that the consequence of sin is *death* (both physical and spiritual).[11]

Since Adam and Eve (the first humans) rebelled against God, all humans are born with a "sin nature." From the time we begin making our own decisions, we begin choosing to do what we know is wrong. We decide to do wrong things or *not to do* right things.

These decisions are *sins*. Both our individual "sins" and our "nature to do sin" make us unfit for living with our perfect Creator. Heaven is perfect because God is perfect. If He allowed sinful creatures to live there, He would no longer be perfect, nor would heaven. Our sin sets us on a road that can only lead away from God, to the place He prepared for Satan called Hell. This is a horrible place, completely separated from the love of God and a place of suffering and *eternal death*.

So, all humans have an urgent need to be saved from their sins that keep them on the path to eternal death. How could this need be met? The cure couldn't come from humans. Man's sinful nature doesn't want to obey God. We would have always selfishly followed our own wills rather than God's.

Fortunately, our perfect Creator is also perfectly loving and merciful. He couldn't just ignore our sin. That would have betrayed His attribute of justness. *But... He could pay the penalty of our sins Himself.* John 3:16, one of the most well-known verses, summarizes...

[11] "The wages of sin is death, but God's gift is eternal life" (Romans 6:23).

> For God so loved the world, that He gave His only son, that whoever believes in Him should not perish but have eternal life.

In a way no one can completely comprehend, God the Father placed the penalty of our sin on His Son. By His death, *Jesus exchanged His righteousness for our sin*. This is the "good news" (gospel) revealed by the New Testament! God in mercy provided a way to save us from eternal death—the fair penalty for our sin.

However, this loving, graceful act by God didn't automatically save us. To receive His free gift, God decided that a person must truly believe that Jesus's death paid his or her sin penalty. We do this by *faith*. And in another difficult to understand action, even the faith to believe is God's gift! The Holy Spirit somehow "sparks" within us the ability to have faith in Jesus.[12] Once again, Ephesians 2:8 tells us…

> By **grace** you have been saved through your **faith**. And even this is not your own doing. It is the gift of God (Ephesians 2:8).

A person is saved when they personally put their *faith* (trust) in what Jesus has done. Sound too simple? Many people think it is. They feel that surely something else must be done to receive such an awesome gift! Some people spend their whole life trying to *do* things to add to God's gift. They may work for a church, give to the poor, read the Bible and pray for long hours, be kind to everyone… These may all be good things that

---

[12] All three Persons of the Trinity are involved in a person's salvation!

one should do, but God's gift is perfect because His Son was perfect. Nothing we do can make us *more* saved or *less* saved! (Why do you think it's called the *good news*!)

Suppose you give a friend a really nice birthday present. The friend opens the box and says "Well, a present surely should be better than this. I'll go buy some more things to go with it." It must disappoint God when we think the gift of His Son isn't enough to save us.

Is being saved complicated?

The good news of God's gift is a simple idea, yet infinitely valuable. Some people try to make it seem complicated with all types of rules, but that was never God's plan. Sometimes it's confusing because different people have different names for "being saved." Here are some common phrases that people use to mean about the same thing…

- salvation
- trusting Jesus (Christ)
- accepting Jesus
- confirmation
- believing on Jesus
- inviting Jesus into your heart
- being born again
- having your sins forgiven
- becoming a believer

- becoming a Christian
- regeneration
- redemption

I've heard some say that the "steps" of being saved are complicated. What is meant is that several things may happen in a person's mind when they trust Jesus for salvation. For example, someone's actual thoughts might be…

1) "I'm a sinner."
2) "Oh, no! Because of my sins, I will face eternal death."
3) "I don't want to be a sinner."
4) "I believe Jesus paid for my sins."
5) "I accept this gift from God."

When I was saved, I think I did all of these at the same time in about a nanosecond! I was very serious about being saved and simply prayed "Jesus, please save me!" Other people may have these same thoughts over a long time, even years. And some may have a different order. Some people may get very emotional. Others may quietly accept God's gift in their mind. No magic words or rituals are needed. God simply wants honest communication and faith in what Jesus has done.

For some, a simple prayer may be a good way to exercise faith. They may pray something like "God, I know I'm a sinner. I know Jesus died to pay for my sins and can help me turn from them. Because of what Jesus did, please forgive my sin and make me your child."

What exactly does it mean to be a Christian?

Originally, the word "Christian" was used to mean someone was "Christ-like" or simply "a follower of Jesus the Christ." Early followers of Jesus often paid a high price for carrying that name. They were persecuted or killed for being *Christians*.

Unfortunately, today the word Christian has different meanings for different people. Some call themselves Christian because their society somewhat follows a Christian lifestyle. Others go by the name simply because they don't consider themselves atheist, Jewish, Muslim, Hindu, or something else. Many people consider themselves Christian because they try to do good works and agree with some of the ideas that Jesus taught. There are even some people who think they are Christian just because they were raised in a Christian family or had some ceremony done when they were born.

In the truest sense of the word, however, a Christian is one who personally trusts Jesus to forgive their sins and give them eternal life. Furthermore, a true Christian is obedient to the Words of Jesus and the Bible. They are indeed *Christ-like* because they are saved and have a relationship with Jesus the Christ!

What do I do after I'm saved?

Salvation is an extremely important event in the believer's life! God's Word says the person has moved from eternal death to eternal life. The decision determines whether one will spend forever with God in Heaven or without Him in Hell.

But the saved person's eternal life has already begun—here on earth! When you are saved, you're now adopted into God's family as one of His children. And you have a job to do within your new family.

Your number one job is to tell others about what God has done for you. In Jesus's "Great Commission" (his final words before leaving earth) He told us to take the good news to all the earth. This involves living your life in a way that shows Jesus to those who know you. The Holy Spirit will help you "be like Jesus" in your words and actions. Your friends will see that you're different, and they will want to know more about it.

We are also to tell others specifically about what God's Word says about salvation. There are many ways to do this. The first step is to pray that the Holy Spirit prepares others to hear the truth about Jesus and salvation. Then you can share with them what Jesus did in saving you. In this way, you are His *witness*. We don't just tell what Jesus *can do*—we tell what He *has done*!

We also spread the good news by supporting others who go around the world telling of Jesus. God's Word instructs us to pray for these *missionaries* and give money to support them. You may think that one person can't accomplish much, but when we combine efforts with other believers, much more is possible.

And that brings up another very important thing for believers to do. Scripture is clear that God expects us to join with other believers. Even though we might do some things individually, God intends for us to work together. Jesus Himself called this group "His church" and "His body." Some think that belonging to a church is just an option we can choose for occasional preaching and parties. However, the Bible describes the church as a crucial part of the believer's life! We can receive some things better as a *body* than as an individual.

Finally, for the rest of your life on this earth, God will be continually shaping you into the image of Jesus. This is called *sanctification.* The more we live the Christian life as the Bible describes the more our relationship with our Creator grows. Like any other friendship, we grow through experiencing things together. Then someday, the relationship will continue into an eternal adventure with our friend Jesus. God's Word promises that this part of the journey will be even more thrilling and spectacular than its earthly beginning!

Can I lose my salvation?

Over the years, there have been arguments over whether a person can ever be "unsaved" and lose the gift of eternal life God has given them. Much of the confusion comes from a misunderstanding of what salvation really is.

As Scripture tells us, salvation is a gift from God. It isn't based on what we *do*, but on what Jesus *has done* for us. We can't add to this gift, so it would make sense that we can't take away from it. To put it simply, we didn't do anything to deserve the gift—we can't do anything to lose the gift. The issue also depends on the nature of God himself. When the omniscient God gives a gift, it is a permanent one, otherwise, why would He give it? Speaking of the ones He saves, Jesus says…

> I give them eternal life, and they will never die. No one will take them out of my hand. (John 10:28)

So, what about Christians who seem to turn their backs on God, leave the church, and go back to a life of sinning? It's possible for believers to temporarily make bad decisions or fall into sin. Jesus's story of the *prodigal son* tells of a man who arrogantly runs away from his father for a while, but then returns home and asks forgiveness. Jesus said the father forgave the son and welcomed him back again.[13] In the same way, God joyfully welcomes back His children who may fall into sin then come back. Sometimes, even good Christians may be led by the devil into sin, doubt, and confusion, but God will lovingly work to bring them back.

The other possibility is that a person may seem to be a believer, but they have never really trusted Jesus to save them. There are many reasons people do this. Some may just enjoy the social part of church. They claim to be a believer just to fit in. Others may think that they are saved just because their parents are. They grow up in church, do good things, say all the right words, yet never

[13] The story of the prodigal son in Luke 15.

have experienced real salvation. They may even attend church regularly, give offerings, and lead church groups hoping their deeds will earn God's gift. Eventually though, those who *fake* Christianity usually turn away from God and the church and reveal their true nature.

The very good news for people in this situation is that God still loves them! His free gift is still offered if they will place their trust in what Jesus has done for them.

ABOUT THE CHRISTIAN LIFE...

What am I?

There's a short cartoon about the beginning of Olaf the snowman from Disney's *Frozen*. The little snowman suddenly realizes he's a conscious being and wonders where He came from and what He is. You may have had similar thoughts. What am I? How did I get here? Why am I here? That's good! It means that you're a thinking person with a desire to know about things.

You may have heard theories about what humans are and how we got to where we are now. Some naturalists believe we are just evolved animals with oversized brains, able to ask questions about our world. These people would say that we are simply chemical machines consisting of cells and organs and such that have been evolving randomly for ages. They would conclude that we are just "accidents" caused by mindless evolution and that we really have no purpose.

The Bible gives a completely different explanation. God says we are special beings, created in His image and made to have a relationship with him. It tells me that I am purposely made to glorify my Creator and to share a loving relationship with him.

My Spirit, the real me that will live forever, is now living in a physical body that is made of molecules and existing in a physical world. The apostle Paul says that my physical body (the one I see in the mirror and the one that lives in the physical world) is like a tent that the real "me" (a spirit) is now living in.[14] My *tent* (body and brain) is physical (atoms, molecules, and energy), but the real conscious *me* is spiritual (*not* atoms, molecules, and energy).

A good way to think about it is: *I don't have a soul, rather I am a soul who lives in a body.*

What is my purpose in the universe?

Every human who thinks has pondered this question. The Bible gives a clear answer. In the words of an old Christian creed, our purpose is to "glorify God and enjoy Him forever."[15]

Perhaps the most important question in life, the simple answer is overlooked by so many. For reasons only God Himself knows, He created humans to be His "image-carriers." Like mirrors, we somehow reflect God's nature, and this brings honor to Him.

But this is by no means a selfish act of God. Believers will spend eternity enjoying the unlimited treasures of God. Scripture says we will *rule* with God. We will *do things*! Adventurous things. Creative things.

---

[14] 2 Corinthians 5:1-8

[15] Westminster Shorter Catechism

Important things. And the joy will never wear off. Even this glorifies God since it reveals him to be good, merciful, generous, and the source of all good things.

If God created a good world, why are things so messed up?

The first book of the Bible, Genesis, tells about God creating the world. We would expect a perfect being to create a perfect world, and according to Scripture, that's just what God did. After each creation event, God even declares "This is good."

But the creation of humans, was a unique event. If the purpose of humans was to reflect the image of God and have a relationship with him, then these beings would have to be free to choose to love. Would you want your friends to be your friends because they had no choice? Who wants robots for friends? In order for love and friendship to exist, the giver of love has to be free to *give* or *not give* love. Only love that is freely given is real love.

But that involves the possibility that someone might not choose to give love or to obey. In a similar way, that's what happened with Adam and Eve, the first people created by God. At first, this couple lived in the garden at Eden in perfect friendship with their Creator. The Bible says Adam and Eve spent time with God every day in the garden.

But as an indicator of whether their friendship and obedience were true, God told them that a certain tree in the garden had fruit that they must not eat. Adam and Eve now had a real test of their love for God. Did they really love him, or would they decide to disobey Him if a selfish opportunity came?

Satan, in the form of a serpent, convinced them that it would be better to disobey God and eat the fruit. The serpent led them to question whether their Creator really had their best interest in mind. Unfortunately, Adam and Eve decided it was better to ignore God and try to improve themselves without His help. They ate the fruit. The first sin was done…

God then allowed the couple to experience the consequences of turning away from the perfect plan of a perfect God. A world without God's goodness is a world that doesn't work well at all. From what the Bible says, the effects were immediate. Living things began to die. Things began to fall apart. Nothing worked perfectly anymore.

This event is called the *Fall* or the *Curse.* Instead of a world that reflected the perfection of its Creator, it now showed all the signs of a world separated from God. The entire universe headed toward *entropy*, a scientific way of saying decay, deterioration, and death. The Fall also affected all of Adam's and Eve's descendants (that's us). We inherited their fallen sin nature.

From a scientist's point of view, I'm amazed by the complexity and beauty of how nature works. And this is after things have been messed up by the Fall! I can't imagine a perfect world without death and decay, but we know that was God's original plan. Thankfully, God is merciful!

Immediately after the Fall, He gave the promise that a "seed" of Adam and Eve (one of their descendants) would someday reverse the effects of the curse and redeem not only the physical world but fallen humans as well.[16] We now know that this promised *Messiah* was Jesus. Although we don't see it yet, His death on the cross redeemed the cursed world. God's Word tells us that right now it's as though the whole world is "groaning" as it waits for the full effect of this redemption.[17] At a future time, Jesus will officially "reset" the creation back to its original state.

Unlike other religions, the hope of Christianity is that a "messed up" world will eventually be made right again. Since I have a mind that's also affected by the Fall, it's hard to imagine what a perfect world will be like, but I can certainly say "Bring it on!"

How do I know what God wants me to do with my life?

You rush into the classroom and take your seat just as the bell rings. Everyone looks expectantly at the teacher, waiting for the class to begin. But she just stands at the front of the room silently…

You raise your hand and ask, "What are we supposed to be doing?"

The teacher answers, "There will be a test tomorrow, and you should do things to prepare."

"But what things?" you ask.

---

[16] Genesis 3:15

[17] Romans 8:19-23

"I'm not going to tell you," the teacher says. "But you need to be prepared for the test!"

What kind of teacher is that? Why would a teacher not want to tell her students what she wanted them to do?

Sometimes, it's easy to think of God as a silent teacher. We expect Him to lay out exactly how He wants our lives to go, but He doesn't. The Bible assures us that we were made for a purpose. It clearly encourages us to seek "God's will" for our lives. So why doesn't He just tell us *exactly* what to do?

Many books have been written about "finding *God's will* for your life." It's a topic about which many people feel frustrated, especially young people who seriously want to know the path God wants them to take for college, marriage, and their career. Why does God's will often seem so mysterious? It's important to remember: *God very much wants you to know His will.* Why would He want to hide it from you?

The answer is, He *wouldn't.* However, there are reason why God's will sometimes seem to be hidden…

Timing. I enjoy hiking mountains. When I stand at the base and look toward the peak, thousands of feet above, I might want to give up before I start. But if I start the climb, focusing on one step at a time, it seems much more reasonable. In the same way, God usually reveals His will one step at a time. This allows me to learn and grow gradually. The experiences learned in one step prepare me for the next. I develop a relationship with God as I trust Him to show the next step. Remember, He is more concerned with what we *are* in life than with what we *do* in life.

Fear. Many years ago, my church was visited by a missionary couple from a very primitive region of the world. After listening to their stories, I was scared… What if God wanted me to go to a place with mosquitoes, typhoons, and no electricity? Was I willing to make such a sacrifice?

Many years later, here I am, never having been sent to the place I dreaded. Yes, I have experienced a few mosquitoes and several other trials. I've noticed, however, that God may call us to make sacrifices, but He always equips and prepares us beforehand. He typically gives us the *desire* and the *courage* to make the sacrifice, so that even though we may experience difficulties, there is joy and fulfillment in following His will. In most cases, if God is calling you to a specific task, He will give you the desire to do it and will usually take away some of the fear.

Disobedience. Among other things, Scripture tells us to be honest, obedient, loving, forgiving, and pure. These are God's will in *every* path in *every* life. If my life path goes against these, or any other principle taught in God's Word, *I am on the wrong path and not doing God's will!*

If I am not obedient in the clear things God tells me in His Word, why should I expect Him to reveal more of His will? I must first obey His revealed will before I receive more guidance.

God's will for your life isn't meant to be mysterious. If you are facing decisions that will change your life significantly, you should certainly pray and study God's Word about that area. If you are a sincere, obedient, listening believer, the Spirit will direct your steps. Wait for opportunities to open (or close). And it's certainly good to talk with godly people in your family or church. God very often places wise people in our lives just for that purpose!

Is it my *heart* or my *mind*?

When you get a valentine is it usually a heart or a brain? Duh…

We've learned a lot about human anatomy and physiology in the last few decades. Obviously, our thoughts and emotions are associated with our brains and not the organ that pumps blood around our bodies.[18] Still though, older literature and even our speech refers to the heart as our *soul* or center of being.

Scripture also speaks as though the heart was our thinking and feeling organ. This doesn't mean that there are mistakes in the Bible, rather, the writers sometimes used metaphors and ideas of the day. It's still common in many languages to hear "I feel it in my heart," or "He has a heart of gold," although we know it's our thoughts and not our heart.

[18] We're actually not even sure how the brain is associated with the conscious spirit. My brain seems to be connected with the real "me," but there is still something different about my physical brain and my supernatural spirit.

What if I doubt my salvation, the Bible, or even God?

Being a believer doesn't necessarily mean that you'll believe 100% of what the Bible says 100% percent of the time! You're a human. Unlike God, you don't have unlimited understanding of things. *God understands your weaknesses and limitations*.

Even the strongest Christians have doubts at times about all types of things. After one of the greatest displays of God's power of all times, Elijah doubted whether God would continue to help him.[19] At Jesus's death the disciples were full of doubt and anxiety.

More important, God isn't worried by our worrying. When I worry that God may not do what He promises, He isn't shaking His head saying "What will I do now! He doubts me!" My Creator is always bigger than my doubt.

I've found that God can often use a little bit of doubting in a good way. When I doubt something, I get a desire to learn more about it. It makes me want to find an answer in God's Word. Sometimes, doubting causes me to pray more and depend on God more. These are good things!

When the disciple Thomas doubted that the previously dead Jesus was really in front of him, alive and well, Jesus didn't criticize him for doubting. Instead, Jesus showed him the evidence of His wounds and told him to see for himself.

[19] 1 Kings 19

Some believers go through times of doubting things that the Bible says. I would guess that most Christians have at some time doubted whether God even exists. *God can handle any doubt you have.* He's isn't surprised or alarmed.

When you have doubts about anything, the best thing to do is share your concerns. This is one of the reasons we are to be members of a church. Other believers can pray for you, listen to you, and encourage you. They may even tell about how they conquered the same doubts.

Also, look for *apologetic* resources that address your specific questions. It's very unlikely that you're the first person to ever have your question! Many good apologists have good answers to your questions, based on solid biblical and logical truth.

Finally, pray and keep studying God's Word. A close relationship with God can push away even the darkest doubt.

Why should I pray if God already knows everything?

The easy answer—because God said to. Surely, He wouldn't ask us to do something unnecessary and useless. So, let's do some thinking…

One Scripture passage tell us "You do not have, because you do not ask."[20] This means that God knew of

[20] James 4:2-3

a need (he's omniscient) but didn't provide the need because He wasn't asked (in prayer). How is that possible if God is loving, generous, and willing to provide for His children?

This is another *paradox* related to God.[21] Somehow, even though He *could* work without us, and He *could* give us what we need before we ask, He doesn't always. In His wisdom, God amazingly and graciously allows our "input" into His actions. What a privilege! (And responsibility.)

Some have also suggested that prayer grows our relationship with God. Just as your parents will probably take care of your needs without your asking, isn't it better to sit down together and talk it over? In praying for our needs, we learn to agree with God about them. Often, I get a clearer picture of what I need as I pray.

Digging Deeper… It's interesting that Jesus Himself prayed often. The 2nd Person of the Trinity prayed to God the Father. This was more than simply an example for us. The prayers of the *man* Jesus were significant in the outcome of God's plans, as are ours. In the hours before His crucifixion, Jesus agonized in prayer and even asked the Father to bypass His future suffering if there were any another way to pay for human sin. God the Father did answer that prayer by showing there was *no other way.*

---

[21] A paradox is something known to be true, yet we can't see how.

How should I pray?

When you ask this question, you're in good company! The Apostles asked the same thing of Jesus. In Matthew chapter 6, He gave them a "model" prayer to show them the basics.[22] These aren't "magic words" or the phrases we are *always* to pray, but a simple example of the attitude and content of the typical prayer. It's okay occasionally to pray the exact words of this model prayer, but remember, the important thing is whether we are sincere about the words we are speaking.

In its basic form, a prayer to God should be like speaking with a friend. Should we be that bold—to come to the very Creator of the universe and speak to Him as a friend?

Yes! That's more *good news*! Jesus's sacrifice gave believers the privilege of coming directly to God and speaking to Him like a father or close friend. How would you speak to your friend? Memorized phrases? Vague requests? No! You speak with a friend respectfully, but very *personally* and very *specifically*. It's a conversation with someone who knows you and they know you.

Prayer is so much easier than most people try to make it. Even when we have trouble expressing ourselves in prayer, we are promised that the Holy Spirit will take our confused thoughts and present them clearly to the Father.[23] The important thing is to pray often and

---

[22] This is often called "the Lord's prayer" or "the apostles' prayer."
[23] Romans 8:26.

sincerely. The Bible promises that your prayers will "accomplish much!"[24]

Should I wait for God to do it, or handle it myself?

That's a very good question, and one that is asked by many people. We have many examples in Scripture of God telling His people to stand back and let Him work. But we also see God instructing His people to "get busy" and do His will. The answer is *both*…

Those paradoxes keep popping up, don't they? Somehow, believers rely on God to work through us and for us by His Spirit. But we're also expected to obey Him and work for Him. When do we wait, and when do we go? Should I "let go, and let God…" or push forward and act?

A good example of waiting was Abraham. God promised that even in his old age he would have a son. Abraham decided to "help" God out, so he had a child by the servant Hagar. But God intended to give the son through Abraham's wife, Sarah. In the end, there were two sons—Ishmael and Isaac. One was God's way, the other wasn't. Abraham's decision not to wait caused lots of problems!

Yet we have the new Testament parable of a man who was entrusted by his boss with money. Instead of using money to make more money for the boss, the man

[24] James 5:16.

hid it. In this story, Jesus criticized the man for not trying harder.

This paradox is solvable, however. Suppose you've just been assigned a major history project. You need to come up with a topic that fits the assignment guidelines. Do you wait for God to just pop a topic into your mind? Will the topic miraculously appear spelled out in your cereal bowl? Maybe, but He likely intends for you to do some digging. Check online for interesting ideas. See what your friends are doing. Look through your textbook.

On the other hand, imagine your little sister is sick in bed. Does God want you to rush in with some treatment from the medicine cabinet, or should you pray and wait for your parents' or the doctor's advice? Very often the plan of action is obvious. Here are some general guidelines to help determine whether you should wait for God to work or dive in yourself (or both). Remember, these are *only* guidelines…

- Is there a clear Scriptural principle that says what to do in this situation? Then do it!
- If in doubt, pray about it. Find a principle in the Bible. Ask another believer for advice.
- Every situation is different. Sometimes it's good to wait for God to move. Sometimes it's good to go forward. After doing all the above, listen for the leading of the Holy Spirit.

Some decisions are just plain tough. But God specializes in leading His children! It's always appropriate to trust Him.

"Trust the Lord with all your heart and don't just depend on what you understand. Obey Him and He will guide your path" (Proverbs 3:5-6).

What is my spiritual gift?

In the New Testament, the church is often compared to a *body*. In the same way that fingers, toes, legs, and noses all work together for the good of the whole human body, members of a church have different functions that all work together for the common good.

Obviously, many organizations and businesses are like this. Different people use their specific skills to accomplish goals. But it's more than this in the church. Yes, we are all born with (or learn) various skills and talents, and these are quite useful in the church. However, the Bible describes spiritual gifts as something different. When one is saved, he or she supernaturally receives certain gifts (abilities) from the Holy Spirit.[25] The Spirit assigns the gift (or gifts) so that the local church can function. It will have all the *parts* that a body *needs*.

Scripture provides lists of gifts in several places.[26] Here are some examples…

---

[25] Even though this is a supernatural working of the Holy Spirit, it isn't necessarily like being zapped with some superpower! The gift is real (and supernatural), but usually isn't sensationalized. Your gift may even seem like a natural talent.

[26] Passages mentioning spiritual gifts: 1 Corinthians 12:4-11 and 27-28, Romans 12:6-8, and others

Prophesy - Speaks God's truth boldly.
Evangelism - Shares the gospel enthusiastically.
Pastoring - One who cares for the local church.
Teaching - Makes the Word of God clear.
Wisdom - Applies spiritual truth to practical situations.
Knowledge - Understands spiritual truths.
Faith - An extraordinary ability to depend on God.
Healing - Helps others be physically and spiritually well.
Discernment - Able to tell the difference between the Spirit of God and evil spirits.
Administration - Organizes and offers guidance.
Service – A heart set on helping others.
Encouragement – Strengthens others.
Giving - One with the ability to give cheerfully.
Leadership - Leads others toward a goal.
Mercy- Loves the unlovable.

Your spiritual gift may be similar to a talent you already had, or it could be something completely new to you. You may have been given more than one gift. Some gifts may *seem* more important (or get more attention), but all gifts were wisely given by the Spirit for an important role. *Your church needs your gift—that's the way it works!*

Remember, your spiritual gifts are intended to build and serve the church body and to help accomplish its mission. True gifts should never lead to arrogance or jealousy among members. Even if you are a young believer, you still have spiritual gifts. As you grow in your faith, take note of how you serve in the church. What do you feel comfortable doing? What do you feel enthusiastic about doing? In which church roles do you seem to be successful? In which roles do others tend to think you are "gifted?"

As you learn more and more about your spiritual gifts (and your natural talents), make them available to your church. If you think you *might* have a particular gift and it doesn't seem to work out, don't give up. Reconsider! Ask others to help you see your gifts.

And even if you don't have a certain gift, don't think you can't express that attribute. You may not have the gift of evangelism, but you can still lead a friend to Jesus! You may not have the gift of encouragement, but you shouldn't be *dis*couraging and rude to everyone!

Does God need my money, talents, and time?

The Bible makes it clear that God deserves our all! We owe Him our very being and we should offer all our resources willingly, thankfully, and happily out of a loving relationship. But does God *need* our help?

The quick answer is *no*. God is completely self-sufficient with no needs that depend on us or any other creature. This is a hard idea for some since we're often urged to give money and volunteer our time. We may get the idea that God's work won't get done without us. But if we accept the scriptural truth of God's *sovereignty* (his total independence) we understand that His kingdom won't fall apart if we fail in our responsibilities!

Having said this, however, here's the paradox… *God desires that we join Him in His work.*

When I was building our first house, my children would often be there with me, playing in the sawdust. Often, I would let them "help" drive a nail or position a board. Could I have done it without them? Of course!

The point is, *they were with me*. I enjoyed involving them and I hope they enjoyed it as well. We grew our relationships by doing things together. In the same way, God is more concerned with our relationship than with what we can do for him. He really wants *us*, not our work or money. God actually enjoys it when we work with him, and we enjoy him!

How do I grow as a Christian?

In case you've never seen one, a killdeer is a long-legged bird similar to a sandpiper. Once I discovered a nest of three killdeer eggs in my yard. I was fortunate to be mowing the yard one day when the eggs began to hatch.

The newly hatched babies popped out of the shell and immediately stood on their long, skinny little legs. Within a few minutes, three tiny birds were running behind their mother, pecking at insects, and trying to get far away from me.

God decided that human babies would be quite different. We're pretty much helpless the first months. It takes years for us to be nurtured by our parents and eventually be able to take care of ourselves. Growing as a Christian is the same way. God could have made it so that when one becomes a Christian, he or she gets "zapped" with all the knowledge and wisdom it takes to live a Christian life. However, it isn't that way. Growing from a *baby* Christian to a *mature* Christian is a process that continues for a lifetime.

Even Jesus (as a man) experienced physical and spiritual growth. It's hard to understand just how, but Scripture tells us He "grew in wisdom and stature."[27] God's Word often compares believers to babies who drink milk (learn the simpler spiritual things) and eventually eat meat (learn the more complicated spiritual things).[28]

So, how do I grow spiritually? Remember once again, Christianity is all about a relationship. Our relationship with God grows as we learn more about Him—not just facts about Him but *real familiarity*. We grow in our relationship by spending time, speaking, listening, observing, and enjoying.

Some call these things *spiritual disciplines*. It's unfortunate that the word "discipline" has come to mean a bad thing. In this case, it's something that brings a very good result. Musicians and athletes use discipline to become good at what they do. The discipline of "practice, practice, practice!" leads to their goal.

Spiritual disciplines are things like prayer, Bible reading, and listening to the Spirit. It could also be listening to sermons and worshipping with music. The point is that we need *regular time with God*. And as with any friendship, the more (and the more often) the better!

---

[27] Luke 2:52. Somehow, the 2nd person of the Trinity limited Himself so that He learned gradually just like us!
[28] 1 Peter 2:2.

But couldn't practice (and spiritual discipline) become a drag after a while? Well, yes… I don't pretend that I don't have bad moods. I'm sad to say there are times I don't feel like reading the Bible. Sometimes when I pray, I feel like no one is listening. God understands!

He knows I'm not perfect. I get grumpy. I get lazy. Sometimes this may be a sinful decision. Sometimes it's just my fallen human nature. Obviously, if this mood lasts a while, something is wrong, and I need to ask God to help me change. When I go through times that I don't want to do what I should, I've found the best thing to do is *do it anyway*. When I don't feel like praying or reading the Bible, that's probably the time I need them most!

The really good news is that God wants to have a friendship with you. He enjoys it, and He knows it's best for *you*. And God wants the friendship to grow and get better and better. If possible, try to have a regular time that you can get alone and read His Word, pray, and listen to the Spirit. Make it a habit and a priority. Your friendship with your Creator will grow and grow!

Why should I be baptized?

The word "baptize" means to *immerse* or *plunge* into something. I often *baptize* my cookies in milk before eating them, or I could be *baptized* in a book I'm reading.

In the New Testament, John the Baptizer was immersing his followers in the Jordan River to symbolize that they wanted to turn from ("wash away") their sins and obey His teachings. In a similar way, Jesus asked His followers to show their allegiance to Him by being baptized. Being "buried" in water then "rising up" out of it, symbolizes that a believer is a follower of Jesus who was buried and rose again. It also pictures the fact that our sins have been "washed away" by Jesus's sacrifice.

Various denominations have different views of baptism. Some say that it's necessary for salvation. Some do it to babies and children. Others simply sprinkle water on the heads of believers.

Nevertheless, the Old Testament examples of baptism are clear. In every case, baptism involved immersing the entire body in water. Also, baptism happened *after* the believer had *personally* made the decision to follow Jesus.

Although baptism is very important in being fully obedient to Jesus, it isn't an essential truth that determines salvation. Believers shouldn't divide over these differences although they commonly do. As with other non-essential truths, discussions are good and appropriate, but arguments are not. We should always make it our goal to be true to Scripture, but in a way that doesn't unnecessarily divide us or drive away those with whom we should be sharing the gospel.

Do I have to love everyone?

The English language is odd in some ways. We use the word "set" in over twenty different ways… I set the timer… I'm all set to go… He set the pencil down… She has a set of dishes… We set the record…

The word "love" is much the same. She loves her sister… I love kittens… He loves chocolate cake… I would love to go there…

The languages in which the Bible was written had several words to describe different types of love (or liking something a lot). Sometimes it's confusing when Bible translations in English simply call them all love. There is one biblical word that means friendship. Another one describes a deeper type of friendship that you might use to talk about the bond among your family members. Another biblical love-word means simply to crave something strongly.

Perhaps the most common love-word in Scripture is "agape" (ah-GAH-pay). In a sense, this type of love is more of an attitude than it is a feeling. Agape has been described in several ways…

1) Placing someone's well-being ahead of your own.
2) Unconditional devotion to someone without expecting anything in return.
3) Sacrificial love.
4) Godly love.

Agape love is modeled after the type of love God has shown us…

> "For God so **loved** [agape] the world that He gave His only begotten son…" (John 3:16).

God *chose* to seek our well-being—a decision, not a feeling. His love was a sacrifice. It was given to us even though we didn't deserve it and could never have earned it. The things we might do can never make Him love us any more or any less.

When God's Word tell us to love, it's always the agape type of love. Obviously, we can't make ourselves *feel* certain emotions such as the other types of love. That's why agape love is always an attitude or a choice we make. We *commit* ourselves to seek the well-being of another. And certainly, we may have several types of love for a person. We might love someone with a friendship-love, family-love, and agape-love at the same time.

So, back to the original question—should we love everyone? Yes, we should develop agape love for other people, whether they deserve it or whether we get anything in return. That's how God loves us, and we, His children, should do the same. And since agape-love isn't a feeling, we don't necessarily have to even *like* the person we decide to give this Godly love.

Sometimes seeking the best for someone else might be a sacrifice, but that should never mean we should be abused by someone and excuse it as love. If someone tried to harm one of my family, I might eventually forgive that person and offer agape-love. I hope I could pray that they turn to God and seek His forgiveness and blessings. However, I would probably never allow this person near my family again.

Godly love may be difficult sometimes. When we give agape-love, we are more like Jesus who perfectly displayed it to people who certainly didn't deserve it. We should model the type of love Jesus gave and show others the nature of agape-love…

> Love is patient and kind and it never envies or boasts. It isn't arrogant or rude, nor does it insist on its own way. Love isn't irritable or resentful. It doesn't rejoice at wrong-doing but rejoices with the truth. Love bears all things, believes all things, hopes all things, and endures all things (1 Corinthians 13:4-7).

Can Christians feel depressed?

As believers, Jesus's sacrifice has made us free from the power of sin. But the consequences of sin—that's a different story.

One day, believers will live in a perfect place with *glorified* bodies that aren't affected by sickness, pain, and death. Until then, this sinful world and our earthly bodies will continue to give us all kinds of problems. Of course, the Holy Spirit helps us in our pain and problems, but they still exist.

Although as a believer my mind has been renewed, my thoughts and emotions also still suffer from the consequences of sin. And even though I have the assistance of the Spirit, I have wrong thoughts about things. I worry. I fear. I get hurt. Sometimes I get so sad it feels like I can't go on.

But I'm in good company. The Bible tells of many people who suffered through periods of deep sadness and depression. Just days after one of his most astounding spiritual victories, the prophet Elijah fell into deep despair, to the point that he wanted to die. Famous church leaders have wrestled with depression, such as Martin Luther and Charles Spurgeon. Even Abraham Lincoln suffered through long periods of sadness and despair.

If you or someone you know is experiencing deep depression or long periods of sadness, it shouldn't be ignored! Start by talking honestly with your parents or your pastor as soon as possible. They may recommend that a counselor or psychologist be consulted. This is nothing to be ashamed of. The Bible encourages us to seek out wise, godly counselors when we're in need.

Sometimes, a counselor may suggest a medical doctor who can treat chemical imbalances in the brain. There are many medications available today that are safe and effective in treating this type of depression. Often, it's good to confront depression from several angles…

- A church leader who can pray with the person and help them deal with spiritual issues.
- A counselor who can identify unhelpful thinking.
- Medications to correct physical issues.

It's important to realize that God doesn't intend for His children to suffer sadness forever! He does, however, want us to deal with the causes of depression and get back to living the life He intended. I so look forward to the time that my totally renewed mind will experience the total perfection of Jesus in His perfect world. Until then, I must lean on Jesus and all the resources He provides to have a pure and healthy mind and body.

Why are some Christians persecuted?

Some people think that when a person trusts Jesus to save them and begins to live the Christian life, all problems disappear. The Bible certainly doesn't teach this.

Yes, every believer has eternal life and can look forward to a joyous "forever" in Heaven where there will be no problems. But God's Word clearly says that in this earthly life we will experience bad things. For now, we have fallen physical bodies. We're born with a sinful nature. We live in a messed-up world. And on top of all this, Satan constantly tries to make us stumble.

The good news is that the believer has the Holy Spirit and the many promises that the bad things that come our way can produce good results. God will even use Satan's evil work to bring about goodness. Still though, believers will experience pain, fear, sickness, and other bad things that all humans experience. These experiences should make us stronger and wiser in God's truth.

In addition, Scripture says that some people will suffer *because they are Christians*. We call it *persecution* when nonbelievers cause believers to suffer, just because they follow Jesus. In fact, Jesus said that since many people would dislike Him, we should also expect them to dislike His followers. It's one of the saddest truths in the Bible. Many don't simply disagree or refuse to accept Jesus—they hate Him.

Christians have been persecuted since the time Jesus first established His church. When the persecution results in death, these believers are known as *martyrs*.

Although you may not see it in your part of the world, there is likely more persecution of believers worldwide today than any other time in history. As our culture changes, you may experience types of persecution because of your faith in Jesus. We should be ready and willing to suffer persecution for following Jesus. God's Word promises that any trials we face on earth will result in incomparable joy in Heaven.[29]

What if a believer takes his or her own life?

Suicide is a tragic decision that saddens God greatly. It is indeed heart-breaking when someone thinks that this is the only way to solve earthly problems.

---

[29] Romans 8:18.

Although suicide isn't an unforgivable sin, it is a sin, nonetheless. Our lives (including the length of our lives) must be in God's hands alone. Suicide says "No" to the plans God has for one's life. The decision robs that person of the joys He has planned for them and the glory He would receive from their life. It causes great sorry and confusion for loved ones and friends, as well as diminishing that person's witness to the power of Christ.

The familiar verse John 3:16 assures us that "God loved the world so much that He gave His Son so that whoever believes in Him will have eternal life." Believers have the sure promise that Jesus gives *life* and helps us *live it*! Trials in believers' lives can be used by God to grow and shape them. There are no problems too great for Jesus to lead us through!

For whatever reason, a person who is considering suicide *is not thinking clearly*. They need help! If you know someone in this situation, you certainly should pray for them, but also talk with a parent, pastor, or counsellor as soon as possible. God's plan is to give the believer hope and a clear mind!

Are all Christians saved?

I saw a news story this week about a man who had pretended to be a medical doctor for over twenty years. The man had never been to college and had no training in medicine yet had treated thousands of patients. Needless to say, his coworkers and patients were in shock after finding out about the deception.

Wearing the name "Christian" doesn't make one a Christian any more than claiming to be a doctor makes one a doctor. Jesus said that after death, many will say to him, "Jesus, I've served you all my life! I'm your follower!" But He will tell them "Leave me. I never knew you."[30] Even among Jesus's disciples, Judas deceived the followers into thinking he was one of them.

There is likely a great number of people in the world today who claim to be Christians but have never trusted Jesus to forgive their sins. Some pretend to be Christian because their family is Christian, others because it helps their business or personal life.

Jesus said we can tell His true followers by their "fruits."[31] Just as we can identify an apple tree because it has apples, we know a true believer because their actions will be those of a true believer. Pretenders may show some deeds that appear godly, but eventually their true "fruit" will show.

How do I know what is true and what is false?

Suppose I told you, "Broccoli is the best tasting food ever!"

I would imagine there are lots of people who would disagree. Some might even say that broccoli is the *worst*

---

[30] Matthew 7:21-23.
[31] Matthew 7:14.

food ever. You might argue that pizza is the best. Your friend might say tacos.

But I still say, "The best tasting food is broccoli!"

And not only do I make that statement, I also say that the statement is *true*.

"Wait a minute!" you exclaim. "What's true for you may not be true for me!" And you would be correct. The flavor of broccoli could be delicious to one person and horrible to another. Flavor is a *preference* and people might *prefer* different things. A statement about your preference could be true for you but not true for me.

Now let me make another statement: "Broccoli is a plant." Suppose one of your not-so-scientific friends says "No, broccoli is an animal." Your friend is not arguing about a preference. No matter how much this person *prefers* to call broccoli an animal, the *facts* about what we can observe about broccoli tell us it's a plant.[32]

So, some things are *relatively true* and others are *absolutely true*. Our preferences and opinions may be relatively true which means they are true for some but maybe not for others. However, things that are absolutely true are true because they are based on reality. Absolute truth is true even if most people don't believe it. It's even true if *no people* believe it.

There is much disagreement in the world today over which beliefs are relatively true and which are absolutely true. In fact, most people question whether *any* truth is absolute. This idea, called *relativism*, claims that most or *all* beliefs are relative. So, if I say something

---

[32] Some may still argue that our facts about plants and animals (or reality in general) are wrong, but the Bible, science, and common sense in general assume that that facts about the world around us are knowable and consistent. We'll stick with that belief.

is true, a relativist would say, "It may be true for you, but not for me."

For example, I think that knocking you down and taking your lunch money is wrong. Not only does it just seem wrong to me, God gives a commandment in His Word that says "You shall not steal!"

However, a relativist might say that that shouldn't be a strict rule. What if someone was very, very hungry and had no money? Shouldn't they be allowed to steal someone else's lunch money? Or what if someone's little sister was very, very hungry? Would that now make it right to steal?

You can see how the idea of absolute truth can lead to some sticky disagreements. You may even be thinking of some other extreme situations in which stealing would be okay.

This is where an important faith principle comes into play. The Bible teaches that when God gives a clear rule about anything, that is an *absolute truth*. God is the ultimate "decider" of what is true or false, good or bad, right or wrong!

We also know that God's nature is to be perfectly loving, righteous, unchanging, and fair. He can't possibly be wrong in any rule that He sets forth. So, even if my mind seems to find something wrong with God's truth, the wrongness must be in my mind.

This is a difficult idea, even for some believers. It also goes against what our culture says. Most people want to believe that God's clear principles can have all types of exceptions. (Usually this is because we want to be the exception and have things our own way.)

It takes courage to stand on God's truth. There is no promise that it will always be easy or popular. It is, however, absolutely true that God expects us to know His truth and to stand in it…

We know that the Son of God has come and has given us understanding, so that we can know Him who is true. We are in Him who is true, in His Son Jesus. He is the true God... (1 John 5:20).

Obviously, I'm not free to interpret God's Word from my own views and desires. I must be certain of what God actually says through the Bible. If I claim that something is *absolutely* true, I must know *absolutely* that God said it! This can only come from the spiritual discipline of studying God's Word and keeping a strong relationship with Him.

How do I know what is good and what is bad?

Is it good to be kind to your friends? Is it bad to hurt an innocent child?

You likely didn't have to think long about either question. Isn't it interesting that you seem to know the difference between good and bad things without having to be taught? Yes, you were probably taught things you should do and things you shouldn't do, but it was because you chose not to do the right thing—not because you didn't know.

Philosophers have spent a lot of time thinking about that. Humans (unlike other animals) seem to have a built-in sense of right and wrong. Some claim it's just a result of evolution within a society. (If humans weren't kind to their friends, our species would have died off.)

I feel it's something more, and God's Word backs up that feeling. Scriptural explains that we were created in *God's image*. God knows right from wrong and so do His image-bearers. Romans chapter 2 says that even those who haven't heard God's law, still know that it is there, telling them right and wrong. God has "written His law" on human hearts.

We often call this a *conscience*. Some consider it strong evidence for an intelligent Creator, since it would be hard to imagine evolution producing such a sense. Atheists and other naturalists are at a loss to explain why they feel things are right or wrong but have no reason for the feeling.

In addition to a conscience, believers have another "internal guidance system." When I put my trust in Christ, God put His Spirit inside me. The Holy Spirit is even more specific in guiding me to know good/bad, right/wrong, and true/false…

> When the Spirit comes, He will guide you into all truth. (John 16:13).

Is it wrong to judge others?

I was once in a church service when I began hearing a man a few rows back whispering. Then he began mumbling out loud.

"How rude!" I thought. "This is a very important sermon, and this guy is ruining it!"

Then he began making sounds as though he was mocking the speaker. I was becoming angry. I got up and walked back to his seat. Immediately I saw the real situation. This man was having a seizure of some sort. The good news was, he was taken for treatment and ended up okay.

The bad news was, I acted on my bad interpretations. I judged him to be an insensitive jerk, and that certainly was not the case!

It's a very popular idea in the world today that "tolerance" = "good" while "judging" = "bad." Is it safe to always assume that what seems bad might be good? Is it always bad to judge the behavior of someone? A better question might be "What does God's Word say about judging other people?"

When a judgment is made about someone today, many people would shout "Wait, didn't Jesus say 'Judge not?'"[33]

Unfortunately, the rest of the passage is typically left off. He actually said, "Judge not, or you will be judged." In the context of this entire passage, it would be interpreted more like "If you judge someone else, make sure you aren't guilty of the same thing." Jesus goes on by using *hyperbole* (an exaggerated example), "Why would you try to advise someone about a speck in their eye, when there's a huge stick in your eye?"

This passage is about being a hypocrite, not whether judging is right or wrong. Other verses give much better insight about judging. In John 7:24, Jesus says "Judge the right way—not by mere appearance." So, Jesus indicates there is a proper way to judge another person.

---

[33] Matthew 7:1

God's Word tells us to stay away from false teachers. We can only do this by judging their words by the truths of Scripture. We are also expected to help others who are trapped in sinful practices. Again, this can only be done if we first determine (judge) someone's behavior as being sinful.

There are three problems to avoid when we might feel the need to judge. First, we can judge only another person's *actions*—not their *motives*. The Bible defines certain actions that are clearly wrong (lying, stealing, lusting, murdering, etc.) God has *already* judged sins such as these, and we are justified in agreeing with Him when a person commits those sins. However, we are not justified in judging *why* a person acts in a sinful way. Only God Himself knows the mind and motives.

Second, we should only judge that which God has indeed *clearly judged*. For example, stealing is always a sin, but what about video games? I know a person who believes all video games are sinful. There may be some truth in what he believes. It's quite possible that video game-playing might cause someone to waste time which could be spent on more godly pursuits. Or a case might be made that video games make the player more violent. Whatever the belief, video game playing in itself isn't something *clearly* judged in Scripture. God is able to judge these situations, but I'm not.

Finally, if I feel good or superior when I notice someone sinning, I am not judging the *right* way that Jesus described. God's children are saddened by sin and want others to repent and stop sinning. Judging another person's sinful behavior is for a clear purpose—to help that person stop sinning. The attitude "I'm-better-than-you" has no place in judging the actions of others. We must always deal with others in love, gentleness, and a helpful, humble spirit.

Why do Christians still do bad things?

As mentioned previously, not everyone who claims to be a Christian is a true believer. We would expect "bad fruit" from a pretend Christian. But it's very possible for true believers to sin. Having our sins forgiven doesn't take away our sinful nature. Believers may fall into any sin at any time.

When I sin, it doesn't mean I lose my salvation or that I am less loved by God. Jesus's sacrifice paid for all my sins past, present, and future. However, my relationship with God is affected—not from His side, but from mine. My guilty heart won't allow the close friendship with Him that I had before I sinned.

The good news is that when we confess our sins to God He is always "faithful and just to forgive us" (1 John 1:19). We have God's promise that He will restore our relationship with him.

Will God's patience ever run out? As humans, our patience may seem limited. But God's Word says He will forgive us "70 x 7 times." This is a way of saying He will *never* stop forgiving as long as we keep confessing and sincerely trying to turn from our sins.

But doesn't that make sinning easy? If God will always forgive me, isn't that just a free ticket to keep on sinning? When asked that question, the Apostle Paul explained that a true believer will not *want* to keep on sinning. On-going, long-term sin isn't the nature of a true believer. The Bible encourages believers to deal with sin quickly. Jesus's sacrifice gives us "a new life" (Romans 6:4). The Spirit helps us to turn from sin and stay away from situations that tempt us.

Does God want me to pay for my sins?

In the Hindu religion and others, there is the belief that to reach the highest level of joy (sort of their version of heaven) a person's good deeds must outweigh their bad deeds.[34] Unfortunately, ideas like this have crept into some Christians' thinking. We hear things like "what goes around, comes around."

To some extent, our earthly systems of law use this philosophy. If I steal something, I must replace it. If I commit a crime, I must "pay my debt to society" by spending time in prison. If I murder someone, I might be expected to pay with my own life! And, in our earthly legal systems, Scripture supports this idea.

However, our sins offend in two ways… If I steal from you, I have not only committed an offense against you, but against a holy and perfect God. Every sin is both a sin against a human(s) and a sin against God. Our earthly laws may require penance (payback) to human victims, but how can I pay back a perfect God?

---

[34] Hindus and New Age groups call this *karma*. Some mistakenly believe that one must be *reincarnated* many times to "pay off" bad deeds.

The simple answer is *I can't*. Nothing that I can do could ever pay back my offense to the infinite God of the Universe! My infinite offense must have an infinite payback! I could spend the rest of my life doing good deeds every second of every hour, yet still not pay even a small part of my unlimited debt to my Creator. Martin Luther realized the same problem. He spent all his time praying, confessing, reading Scripture, giving, and helping the poor only to realize his *sin debt* remained as heavy as ever.

So, what am I to do? My future is indeed bleak!

Need we say it again? "That's why it's called the Good News!"

As perfect God in the form of a sinless man, Jesus could pay my infinite debt! And not just one sin, Jesus's sacrifice on the cross paid for all my sins—past present, and future. Furthermore, His perfect sinless sacrifice was sufficient for all the sins of all who would ever trust him.

It may sound too good to be true, but as a believer, you will never have to pay for any of your sins. (You couldn't even if you tried.) The perfect, complete sacrifice of Jesus can't possibly be made more perfect or more complete by anything you can do! The Bible says that this is a *gift* from God. Would you try to pay for a gift? That would be an insult to the giver.

But this sort of sounds like we can sin all we want, and God doesn't care, doesn't it? As just mentioned, Paul was asked the same question. He had a good answer… "Of course not! When we trust Jesus to forgive our sins, we are *dead* to sin!"[35]

---

[35] Romans 6:1

Christ not only paid for sin, He defeated it. Certainly, we still sin as believers, but sin does not "possess" us as it once did. We desire to please and obey God. Our service to God is now out of a grateful heart rather than guilt and repayment. We avoid sin because we love God, and He loves us.

What should I do when I sin?

So how do I fix the broken relationship with God caused by my sin?

The first step is to *confess* my sin. This simply means that I sincerely *agree with God…* "Yes, Lord. This was sinful, and I'm sorry for it." Sometimes I've found it helpful to confess out loud to another person who can support me and pray with me.

Next, accept God's forgiveness. Because of Jesus's sacrifice, I'm already forgiven, but it's good to acknowledge it and thank God for it. The Bible assures me that God will put the guilt of that sin as far away as "the east is from the west" (that's a long way!).[36]

Finally, I must deal with the consequences of my sin. Was someone hurt in some way by my sin? If so, I need to ask their forgiveness and repay any debt to them. I should also find ways to prevent the same sin from happening again. If I'm really serious about my confession, I'll not want to do the same sin again. I should pray that the Spirit will help me in this weakness.

[36] Psalm 103:12

Perhaps I'll need to ask others to keep me accountable. Or it could be that I need to remove the temptation—turn off the TV, change who I hang out with, ask someone to monitor my Internet use.

Someday in our heavenly bodies, sin will no longer be a problem. Until then, Scripture tells us that life in this world will be like a race with sins constantly trying to slow me down. To win the race we must…

> …lay aside the sinful distractions which cling so closely, and let's run the race that is set before us with endurance. (Hebrews 12:1)

Why are there people who don't believe in God or choose not to follow Jesus?

God's Word tell us we shouldn't be surprised that many people won't follow or even believe in Him. Jesus Himself said that relatively few people will trust Him for eternal life.[37] God's offer of forgiveness through Christ is open to everyone, but sadly, most stubbornly refuse it.

Some claim to be *agnostic*. They claim they're just not sure enough about Jesus to follow him. Others say they are *atheists* who deny that God exists. There are still others who believe in God, but give reasons for not trusting Jesus for salvation…

---

[37] Matthew 7:13

- "Why would God allow suffering? I can't follow a God like that."
- "I'm nicer than most Christians. Why do I need Jesus?"
- "My good deeds outweigh my bad deeds. Surely I'll get into heaven."
- "Heaven sounds like a boring place. I'd rather not go."
- "All religions will get me to Heaven. I think I'll choose an easy one."
- "I want to have fun first, then someday I'll accept Jesus."

We tend to think that non-believers have intelligent, logical, or scientific reasons for not believing in God or accepting biblical truths. The fact is most non-believers refuse to believe simply because they don't want to. Humans are selfish by nature and want to live their own way. Scripture tells what happened when light (Jesus) came to the earth…

> The light has come into the world, and people loved the darkness rather than the light because their works were evil (John 3:19).

It isn't a *thinking* problem as much as it is a *feeling* problem. Non-believers prefer to keep their sins because they like it that way. It's okay to discuss the logic (or illogic) of a person's disbelief. Ultimately though, when sharing Jesus with others we should present the good news just as the Scripture does and let the Spirit lead them: *God is willing to forgive your sins through His Son Jesus, if you'll turn from darkness to the Light…*

What is faith?

The word "faith" is another word with several meanings. When people say "The Faith" they are usually referring to the Christian religion and all it contains. Usually, "faith" means a type of *trust* in something or someone.

One verse in the Bible says that faith is "the reality of what we hope for, and the proof of what we can't see."[38] However, in most cases, Scripture *illustrates* faith instead of trying to define it.

I've often heard the "wheelbarrow" story used to understand faith:

A certain man lived alone on an isolated mountaintop. When he needed supplies, he would push a wheelbarrow to the nearby town. But to reach the town he would have to push the small cart over a narrow, rickety rope-bridge that spanned a deep rocky gorge. Townspeople would often stop what they were doing and marvel at the skill and bravery of the man as he crossed the dangerous gorge.

One day a stranger in town saw the crowd watching the man cross. He exclaimed to one of the women "The fool is about to die!"

The woman answered, "No, he will make it. He always does."

The stranger said, "Okay. I will pay you $1000 to get in the cart and let him take you across."

[38] Hebrews 11:1

The woman was quick to answer. "No way! I believe he can do it, but I don't *believe* he can do it!"

God's Word shows faith as a type of trust that totally believes. It's a belief that puts my whole self in the wheelbarrow by believing it. But does the Bible say that strong faith is all it takes? Absolutely not!

Had the mountain man tried to cross an imaginary bridge that didn't really exist, it wouldn't matter how strong his faith, or anyone else's was. No amount of faith would save him from falling to his death! The *amount* of faith I have isn't as important as the *dependability* of the thing (person) in whom I place my faith.

How much faith do I need?

Jesus made it very clear that the *amount* of faith I possess isn't as important as the *object* of my faith. Suppose you were skating on a frozen lake. Would you rather have a lot of faith in a one-inch layer of ice or a little faith in a ten-foot layer? Thick ice is reliable even with small faith!

So, faith is only as good as the object (or person) in which it's placed. Faith in Jesus works because Jesus is *completely trustworthy*. Perhaps that's why He said that faith as small as a tiny seed can move a mountain. Even a small amount of true faith is sufficient when placed in an unlimited God.

However, we are encouraged to grow our faith more and more. This doesn't affect the trustworthiness of

God, but it does strengthen our relationship with Him. The better we know Him, the stronger our faith becomes and the more we rely on it. Our faith grows and becomes a strong shield against whatever circumstances we face.

How do I get more faith?

How do we develop a stronger, more effective faith in God? Can a person today have faith like Enoch, Noah, Abraham, Sarah, or Moses?[39]

For a believer, the first act of faith is trusting Jesus for salvation. We still need true faith to live the life God desires. The means through which God provides faith is through his Word, the Bible. Romans 10:17 tells us that "faith comes by hearing God's Word." This means that when we take in the truth of Scripture through reading the Bible, teachers, or preachers, our faith grows.

The townspeople would have never had "faith" in what the mountain man could do had they not seen and heard of him doing it time and again. Reading and hearing God's Word regularly allows us to *know* the object of our faith, Jesus, better and better.

[39] These are some of the people noted in what some call the *Hall of Faith* in Hebrews 11.

What if it feels like the world is out of control?

The book of Job in the Old Testament tells of a godly man who suffered about as many bad things as a person could suffer. At the lowest point in his life, Job wished he had never been born. He believed his life was totally out of control.

There are many lessons we can learn from Job, but for now simply notice that even people who are close to God can feel that the world doesn't make sense. Feelings like this will come and go throughout life. However, be certain about this—as surely as they *come,* they will also *go*. Desperate feelings never last!

But even in the middle of these feelings, we can depend on the truths about God. One of God's attributes is His *sovereignty*. We sometimes say that a king is *sovereign* over his kingdom. This means that he is in control of things within his kingdom.

An earthly king, however, has limited sovereignty. His subjects may obey most of the time, but there is no guarantee they will not break a few rules or even revolt against the king. An earthly king can't always stop disease, storms, or invading armies.

Unlike earthly kings and leaders, the Bible assures that God is *perfectly sovereign*. Being all-powerful (omnipotent) there is nothing that can prevent His will from being done. God will accomplish *everything He wants to do*.[40]

---

[40] Isaiah 46:9-10

This might be disturbing for anyone who opposes God. How can they continue to fight against someone who will *always* win? For believers, however, it is certainly a happy hope! God's children must see this attribute of sovereignty in light of His other attributes. God is also loving, righteous, wise, and just. This means His sovereignty will always work to bring about our greatest good. In other words, even when things may seem out of control, God is in complete control! He loves us and the result will always be to His children's benefit.

Is there any exception to this? Paul gives a very straight answer…

> Can anything separate us from the love of Christ? Shall troubles, or distress, or persecution, or hunger, or neediness, or danger, or attackers? (Romans 8:35).

Since believers are always the focus of God's love, Paul immediately answers his question, "No!"

> In all these things we are more than conquerors through Him who loves us. I am certain that neither death, life, angels, rulers, things now, things to come, powers, heights, depth, nor anything other thing, is able to separate us from the love of God in Christ Jesus our Lord (Romans 8:37-39).

Whenever life seems out of control, read these verses again. Is any possible thing left off this list? No!

So, the reality is *at no time and in no way are believers' lives ever out of God's control*. And if God is in control, only good things will eventually be the result. If you need more encouragement, back up a few verses and we see a similar promise…

> All things work together for good, for those who love God… (Romans 8:28).

Notice two often overlooked points in this popular verse. Yes, God is always in control, but unbelievers have not placed themselves under God's goodness. Only believers who love God can rightly claim His protection.

Also, "all things" will eventually work to bring about "good" for the believer. It doesn't say all things *are* always good in themselves. When I'm in the middle of some of these "all things," they may not seem good at that time. God's promise, though, is that eventually even these bad things will bring about good for me. What a wonderful peace it brings to know that not a single molecule will ever move with His knowledge and permission!

ABOUT SUPERNATURAL THINGS...

Are there really angels?

When we think of heaven, our minds usually go to angels. The word *angel* in Scripture literally means *messenger*. These creations of God are mentioned often in Scripture. They aren't described specifically, but we can piece together a general picture of what they are like.

For example, we know that they were created by God before He created the earth and that there are a *lot* of them. Angels are immortal (they live forever). They have personalities, intelligence, emotions, and wills, just like we do.

Angels are spirits, so they don't have physical bodies like humans. They live in a *supernatural* dimension while ours is *natural*. However, they can and do affect the natural world.[41] Also, there are times when they can appear to people in a natural, physical form—sometimes even as another person.[42]

---

[41] In the book of Job, Satan is able to produce a windstorm.

[42] Hebrews 13:2

Angels have different jobs and ranks. Three of them are named in the Bible—Michael, Gabriel, and Lucifer. Michael is known as an *archangel* (high angel), implying that he outranks others. Lucifer was once an *anointing cherub*, apparently another high-ranking angel, before he rebelled and was cast out of heaven. Scripture mentions other unnamed *cherubim* (plural), as well as beings called *seraphim*.

The images we see of angels in paintings and movies are not exactly the way Scripture reveals them. Those cute, chubby babies flying around make nice Christmas cards, but they aren't actually described that way in the Bible. In fact, the first words of many angels as they appear to people are "Don't be afraid!"

The implication is that they are awesome beings, powerful and commanding, perhaps like warriors. An angel with a flaming sword was assigned to the entrance of the Garden of Eden.[43] Elisha's servant was allowed to see an army of angelic soldiers ready to defend against the invading enemy.[44]

What do angels do? Anything God wants… In Scripture we find them protecting people, announcing events, breaking prison chains, destroying armies, comforting people, and praising God. As awesome as angels are, in our future heavenly home believers will rule over angels. We'll spend eternity with our angelic colleagues carrying out God's work and enjoying His presence!

---

[43] Genesis 3:24

[44] 2 Kings 6

Is there a real devil?

There may have been a real King Arthur who lived in 5th-century England. However, the facts about him have been made so legendary that we might not recognize the real man from all the fanciful stories about him.

The Bible tells of a being called the devil. Because there have been so many "mythical" ideas made up about him, there are people who claim that this being doesn't really exist. Some say "The Devil" is just a term we use for the "combined evil acts" that happen in the world. Nevertheless, God's Word describes him as a very real personality, and it provides some useful warnings about him.

There are several names for this evil being. The word *devil* means "accuser." This refers to one of the things he does. Like a schoolroom tattletale, the devil is constantly pointing out the sins of God's children. Another name is *Satan* which means "enemy." Several Old Testament scriptures indicate that this being was the angel Lucifer. This name "Lucifer" means "shining one."

So, where did Lucifer come from? We know that all things, living and non-living, were created by God. There are absolutely no beings that God did not create. Then did He create an *evil* being?

According to the Bible, Lucifer was one of God's most fantastic creations. Scriptures seem to say that he was the angel in charge of leading the other angels in praising God, maybe like a heavenly choir leader.

Originally, Lucifer was good, powerful, and flawless since God wouldn't make anything evil or imperfect. But God didn't make mindless robots. He wanted the angels (and us) to have the freedom to choose to love and obey him. And if there is freedom to choose obedience, there must also be freedom *not* to choose obedience. In one of the saddest events in cosmic history, Lucifer, used his freedom to oppose his Creator.[45] He arrogantly decided that he would take over as god of the universe.[46]

But remember… *Lucifer is not the opposite of God.* He was created by God. As great and powerful as he is, he has never been even close to God's equal in any way. Satan isn't omnipresent. He isn't omniscient. He isn't omnipotent. He works only as far as God allows.[47]

Then couldn't God do something about him? Actually, He did… God immediately cast Lucifer out of heaven. (We now refer to him as Satan or the devil.) God also created a place to put Satan called Hell. Someday God will permanently put Satan there. The question is, why is He waiting? Why is this devil now free to do evil things in the world?

We've already discussed why God might allow bad things to happen. We don't know all of God's reasons for doing things. Perhaps He allows Satan to do some bad things in order to bring about good results. Martin Luther called Satan "the ape of God" as if Satan is on a leash and is only allowed to do what fits into God's big-picture plan.

---

[45] Ezekiel 28:12-15

[46] Isaiah 14:12-14

[47] See Job 1-2

It's very important that Christians realize that they have a powerful enemy, but that whatever happens, God is still much more powerful and He's always in control…

> Children, you are from God and have overcome, for He [God] who is in you is greater than he [Satan] who is in the world (1 John 4:4).

Are demons real?

Satan has an army of assistants in his evil work. Some people today doubt their existence, but these *demons* are mentioned often in the Bible. The exact origin of these beings isn't spelled out in detail, however, we can be sure that God didn't create evil, and there are no beings that He didn't create. So, like Satan, any spirits who oppose God have *fallen* from their original "goodness."

Several passages seem to tell us that Satan and possibly his angelic followers rebelled against God before the creation of the earth. Some Bible scholars believe that another group of heavenly beings may have fallen around the events of Genesis 6:1-4. Whatever is true, the results are the same. A large number of evil beings now dwell in the unseen, supernatural world. Like their leader, their objective is to oppose God by harassing and misleading humans, especially believers.

Demons seem to be assigned to organized jobs or positions much like the military. The highest level might include the "princes" mentioned in Daniel 10. These high-ranking beings appear to be assigned to entire nations. Paul lists some of the other titles in Ephesians 6. The exact command structure isn't given, but includes "rulers," "authorities," "cosmic powers in this dark world," and "spiritual forces of evil" in heavenly places.

What are these evil beings doing on earth right now?

While we may not understand completely why Satan is free to do evil on the earth, the Bible is clear that he is our enemy and we should guard against him and his demons. As we discuss the devil, don't think for a minute that we are helpless against him. He is a seriously evil enemy, but he was seriously defeated by Jesus's sacrifice on the cross. The devil can only deal with God's children *as God allows*.

Over the centuries, this most evil creature of all time has been turned into just a cartoon or monster-movie character. Medieval artists wanted to show the devil as someone that no one would want to follow, so they portrayed him as a silly being with a red suit, pointy tail, and pitchfork. I'm sure Satan doesn't mind for people to think of him that way. What better way to work secretly than to have people think that you're imaginary or a harmless joker! We acknowledge him as a real enemy, but we have *nothing to fear in him.*

And what is Satan's work today? Jesus summarized it quite well…

> He does not deal in the truth, because there is no truth in him. When he lies, he speaks out of his own nature, for he is a liar and the Father of Lies (John 8:44).

Satan's main strategy in the world today is spreading lies. Lies about God. Lies about God's Word. Lies about Christians. While Jesus is truth "in person," Satan is the personification of "untruth." What a solemn pronouncement on Satan from Jesus: "Father of Lies!"

How does the devil try to spread his lies to me? It could be directly and personally in my own mind. As odd as it might sound, somehow Satan can "place" thoughts in my brain. It's not mind control, but more like "suggestions." It has also been described as a "whisper" or an "impression." Just like a text pops up on my phone, sometimes a bad thought just pops into my head. I think "Wow, where did that come from?"

Since they're in my own head, Satan's whispers usually seem like my own thoughts. And remember, Satan is a master liar. He whispers lies disguised as truth!

And honestly, a lot of my bad thoughts are probably not from the devil. I was born with a sinful nature just like every other person, and unfortunately, I can think up some pretty bad thoughts and lies without any help from the Satan! No one can say "The devil made me do it!" God's power given to us through His Spirit helps us recognize lies (wherever they come from) and turn away from them. We always have a choice of whether to listen to the lies or not. The Bible tells us to "resist the devil" when he tries one of his lies on us.

Another way Satan can "send" lies to you is through other people who are listening to him. There are several "false teachers" mentioned in the New Testament. These men and women were listening to Satan's whispered lies and were leading people away from God's truth.

Throughout the world today, there are many people teaching all kinds of false ideas. These ideas come from Satan and are aimed at leading Jesus's followers into lies and deceptions. And remember, the eevil's lies can be quite tricky. The Bible calls his deceitful tricks "schemes." Some translations use the term "wiles" as in Wile E. Coyote. If you've watched Roadrunner cartoons you know that the coyote never simply waits around for Roadrunner to happen by. He never recklessly chases Roadrunner. No, Wile E. has fancy gadgets and very organized schemes for capturing Roadrunner.

When an army attacks another army, they would never go for the strong points. Successful armies aim for the weak points of the enemy. Satan takes his work seriously and often aims his lies at our most sensitive areas. He may tempt one person with drugs and another with greed. Whatever a person's weakness, there the devil will work.

Believers should expect to be tempted with Satan's lies. And the closer our relationship with Jesus, the more Satan will work to break that relationship. However, this should never scare us or keep us from growing in God's truth. Scripture clearly assures us that "the One living in us (the Holy Spirit) is greater than the one who is in the world (Satan)."

Do supernatural beings ever appear on earth?

We've discussed God's angels—both the faithful ones and the fallen ones. Are there angels at work today? Although some would say the Holy Spirit could easily do their jobs, there is no indication that God has stopped using His divine messengers. Scripture reveals that righteous angels can and do interact with humans.

The New Testament tells of several angelic appearances.[48] Angels may take on a human form. Lot's angelic visitors seemed to look like men (Genesis 19). Hebrews 13:2 says that sometimes we might meet angels and not be able to tell them from ordinary people.

Are there "guardian angels" that watch over and protect us? Jesus seemed to indicate that at least little children have angels assigned to protect them.[49] I did a lot of dangerous things as a child. My angel must have been very busy!

But if righteous angels can appear on earth, can fallen, evil angels do the same? Scripture warns us that Satan can disguise himself as an "angel of light."[50] What appears to be a good being could actually be the devil just pretending to be friendly and helpful. I would guess

---

[48] Angelic appearances: Birth of John the Baptist (Luke 1:5-25), wrestles with Jacob (Genesis 32:22-32), with Gideon (Joshua 5:13-6:27), the fiery furnace (Daniel 3:1-30), leads Peter out of prison (Acts 12:1-19), Gabriel speaks to Mary (Luke 1:26-38), tells the disciples Jesus will return (Acts 1:1-11), announces birth of Jesus (Luke 2:8-20), announces Jesus has risen (Matthew 28:1-10).

[49] Matthew 8:10

[50] 2 Corinthians 11:14

that his demonic helpers can do this, also. This makes sense, though, since Satan's goal is to deceive and lie. His lies would seem more believable coming from a good being than a scary one.

All of this shouldn't worry the believer, however. God is certainly more powerful than any fallen angel. Evil beings may seem frightful, but they can only work within God's permission and plans. We should rest in this truth and at the same time be aware of Satan's trickery.

God's Word encourages us to "examine the spirits to see whether they are from God."[51] Any being or spirit that is truly from God will agree 100% with what the Bible says about Jesus. No matter how good and friendly someone appears, if they change the truth in Scripture, they are *not* from God!

In general, both righteous and fallen angels usually work unseen. Not every weird event is caused by a supernatural being, so there's no need to go around looking for supernatural beings. It should give us great joy and peace to know that the greatest of all supernatural beings, the Creator of everything, is working continuously in the life of every believer.

---

[51] 1 John 4:1-3

How can I defend myself against the devil?

You may be thinking "The devil is such an powerful enemy! How could I ever stop him?" Not to worry! God's Word has a clear strategy for standing against Satan's lies. It encourages us to put on "armor" to protect against the devil's deceptions. Just as a soldier would wear coverings to stop arrows and swords, we are told to put on *spiritual armor* to deflect Satan's "arrows" of deception.[52]

In Ephesians chapter 6, Paul describes several pieces of this spiritual armor…

Helmet of Salvation – Satan tries to make Christians doubt that their sins are forgiven and that they are children of God. He whispers lies telling believers that they need to do more to be saved and that surely God won't forgive all their sins. However, since our salvation depends only on Jesus, the "helmet" is the Bible's promise that Jesus has forgiven our sins and saved us, period!

Shield of Faith – Paul says that Satan's lies are like fiery arrows. But our trust in God and what Jesus has done for us blocks these arrows. For every lie that Satan might tell, there is a promise from God that exposes that lie.

---

[52] Romans 6

Shoes of the Gospel of Peace – A soldier's shoes were very important. If he couldn't hold his position firmly then the other parts of his armor wouldn't work. Christians are at peace with God. He has forgiven our sins and stands beside us. This truth gives us firm footing while we stand against the devil.

Belt of Truth – When an early soldier went into battle, he would pull up the folds of his tunic and hold them inside his belt. When we believe the truths of Scripture, it makes us battle-ready. We aren't bothered by little troubles that Satan throws in our way.

Chest Plate of Righteousness – This piece of armor covered the soldier's heart—a vital organ. Even though the Christian has been forgiven of their sins in general, there are still sins that pop up continually, all the time, every day. Believers must constantly turn away from those daily sins and ask for forgiveness. When I don't live in obedience, dealing with daily sins quickly, my relationship with God suffers. I'm still His child, but I'm not as dependent on God as I should be. My heart is no longer protected, and the devil is able to attack.

Sword of the Spirit – In the Bible, a sword represents God's Word. Notice that this is the only weapon mentioned in the spiritual armor. The weapon that works against Satan is not some magical cross or holy water—it's the Scripture that God has given us. And this doesn't mean it's like a magic phrase we repeat, and the devil runs away. The real truth expressed in the Bible defeats the lies that Satan tells. When he attacks us with a specific lie, there is a specific principle in

God's Word that exposes the lie and destroys it. This is a good reason to study the Bible often and know God's promises. Scripture tells us to "hide God's Word in our heart" so that it's available at a moment's notice. Who wants to go searching for their sword in the middle of a battle!

Did you notice a common idea running through these armor symbols? A good soldier *prepares* for the battle. If an attack is coming, why would he wait for the first arrow before putting on the armor? Wearing spiritual armor doesn't mean being obsessed with always expecting a battle and constantly worrying about it.

But it *does* mean to get in the habit of what we call *spiritual disciple*. Spiritual soldiers should have regular and consistent times for reading the Bible and understanding God's truth. We should pray often and ask for wisdom and understanding. We should learn from others who teach us God's Word. And above all, we should live in obedience to what Scripture teaches, turning away from sin and asking God to forgive us. As Paul says, a good soldier stay ready.

Some Things the Bible Says Satan Does to People…

- Makes us change our plans. (1 Thessalonians 2:18)
- Tempts us. (Matthew 4:10, 1 Corinthians 7:5)
- Keeps us away from truth. (Mark 4:15)
- Causes us to say things. (Mark 8:33)
- Puts lies in our minds. (Acts 5:3)

Is Hell a real place?

Scripture is as clear about Hell as it is about Heaven. It also gives the purpose of Hell—a place for Satan and his fallen angels.

Some say this was a merciful move by God. He could have destroyed Satan and his followers, but instead created a place in which they could pursue what they desired—freedom from God. Although God is omnipresent, in some sense, His presence will be absent from Satan's future home. Satan will indeed be "ruler" of his own limited realm.

As for humans and Hell, God grants the same mercy. Those who wish not to accept Jesus's free gift of salvation are allowed to live with Satan, forever separated from God and His goodness.

I often hear joking about Hell from those who don't take it seriously…

"At least I'll be with my friends!"

"I can finally do all the sinful things I want!"

"Heaven will be boring! I want to be where the party is!"

Jesus viewed Hell quite differently. The place He described is definitely not an eternal party…

- Hell is a place of suffering.
- Once there, there is no leaving.
- All goodness, joy, and righteousness are absent.
- Hell lasts forever.

But to be very clear, God never *ever* intended for people to be in Hell. Jesus died to save us from Hell. The Bible says that the angels are overjoyed when someone turns to Jesus and avoids this terrible place. One of the reasons the gospel is "good news" is that God very much wants us to live in Heaven with Him forever, and not separated by our sins.

What is a miracle?

What exactly is a miracle? We use the word in so many ways.... "It was a miracle that she passed the exam... He miraculously made the goal at the last second... The beautiful newborn is such a miracle... The fever is gone! What a miracle!"

But is it really a miracle every time a rare or "wished-for" event happens? Let's define what a real miracle would look like. Unusual events aren't necessarily miraculous. If you entered your name in a big drawing for a new bicycle, you would probably have a very small chance of winning.

But we know *one* person *will* win the drawing. If you win, it may seem to be a miracle from your view. But from the view of the rest of us, you just happened to be *the one*. Random events may appear to be miraculous when that's just the way math works. As a scientist, I define a real miracle this way...

> Miracle: An event in which a supernatural being changes an earthly situation by altering physical laws.

The resurrection of Jesus was perhaps one of the greatest miracles ever. Normal physical laws would have made Jesus's body decay and turn to dust just like every other dead body. But God (a supernatural being) changed these laws and put life back into dead cells.

Jesus Himself worked many miracles. The laws of math and physics would say that a little bit of bread and fish would feed just a few people. Although Jesus was fully a man, He was also fully God, and His supernatural nature was able to change these laws and make a *little* equal a *lot*. Who would imagine that a basket of food could feed thousands!

Jesus also changed physical laws to walk on water, calm storms, heal the sick, and raise the dead. Was this some kind of magic show to entertain people? Absolutely not! Even though people were amazed by His miracles and many benefitted from them, the main reason Jesus performed miracles was to show who He was—God in human form. He said that we can believe His teachings because His miracles reveal Him as God (John 10:38). Some of the followers of Jesus also worked miracles and for the very same reason. The truth of their teachings was verified by their power to do the miraculous.

Can miracles happen?

Some *naturalists* deny that miracles actually happen.[53] There are also Christians who believe biblical miracles had natural explanations and didn't need supernatural acts. *Deism*, in particular, is the belief that God created the universe then just let it go without interfering in any way.

I meet many Christians who seem embarrassed by Bible miracles. They feel that belief in supernatural

[53] *Naturalism* says that only the natural world exists and there is no supernatural world—no God, spirits, or afterlife.

intervention makes us seem old-fashioned or crazy to the rest of the world. But doesn't it make sense that One who is powerful enough to create the universe out of nothingness could also alter His creation whenever He wished? Which is easier—feeding thousands with a basket of fish and bread or creating an ocean full of fish and the DNA of a wheat plant?

The answer is neither. God can do a "big" miracle as easily as a "little" miracle! But obviously, miracles are very rare. God's universe is incredibly complex and orderly. It does very well in working by itself like a well-designed machine. A person could live their entire life without witnessing a direct miracle, and God is no less God!

Nevertheless, we should not doubt that God *can* work a miracle any time and any way He pleases. We should boldly believe that miracles were as real as any other event recorded in the Bible.

How do I know a miracle when I see it?

Many people today claim to have experienced miracles. As we have seen, miracles are probably very rare, although God can certainly work miracles as He pleases.

When miracles occur in Scripture, it's never like "Hey, wouldn't a miracle be great right now!" Instead there is always a clear purpose that usually is even more important than the miracle itself.

For example, when Jesus fed thousands with a basket of food, it was more than just filling hungry tummies. Jesus was always about teaching His disciples. They would be the ones to start the spread of the gospel to the world. They needed first-hand experience in what God is like and what He can do. If ever they doubted that God could provide the needs of His people, the disciples could think back to the little basket.

When Jesus raised Lazarus from the dead, of course this was beneficial to Lazarus himself. But it was much more than just a kindness to His friend. The big lesson for all who witnessed this miracle was that Jesus even has power over death. If Jesus can solve the biggest problem we have in this life, surely he's able to deal with our little worries!

So, the best way to tell whether something today is a true miracle is to compare it with Bible miracles. Here are some things that all biblical miracles had in common…

- Although God may have used people to do the miracle, there was never a question that it was God's power.
- Those who received the miracles were helped, but biblical miracles were mainly meant to support what the Bible says about God.
- Miracles never went against Scripture or added new truths.
- The result happened immediately and there was no doubt it was real (not like some kind of trick).

Compared with biblical accounts, many modern "miracles" are clearly false. God *can* and *will* use miracles as He pleases, but we should be careful about claiming something as miraculous and guard against those who might try to trick us for their own gain or reputation.

Do I become a ghost or angel when I die?

All through history, people have wondered what happens to us after death. It's interesting that even those who don't believe in God or anything spiritual seem to believe that life continues after death. I believe this is because God has "placed eternity in our hearts."[54] We seem to know deep down that some part of us will live forever. The Bible is very clear about what happens after this life. Our spirits (the real us) will go to one of two realms—Heaven or Hell.

Somewhere, either in our mythology or Hollywood, two wrong ideas came about. The first was that after death the spirit doesn't quite know what to do. It hangs around and "haunts" its former dwelling as a ghost. The typical ghost story is that these bodyless souls wander about trying to take care of "unfinished business" or seeking revenge. This myth is so popular that even many Christians believe it.

But nowhere in Scripture does it even hint that spirits of the dead remain on earth. The Bible assures that our spirits go immediately to their destination of

[54] Ecclesiastes 3:11

Heaven or Hell.[55] In Jesus's story of Lazarus and the rich man, we also find that spirits of the dead (those of unbelievers) aren't allowed to return to the earth.[56]

Even more unbiblical, some have the idea that at death a person's spirit becomes an angel. This may make a good story for movies and cartoons, but it's completely foreign to God's Word. Angels are messengers of God created before the earth and humans.

Believers need not worry about their future homes or the state of their departed loved ones who have trusted Jesus. Nor should we be concerned that spirits of the dead may be haunting certain places. God is in control of every being whether living or dead and He has a specific place prepared for each one.

Are there such things as ghosts?

The idea of ghosts is common in almost every human culture. TV, movies, and books are filled with friendly ghosts, scary ghosts, ghost whisperers, and ghost hunters.

According to the storyline, ghosts are the spirits of humans whose bodies have died. These spirits supposedly wander the earth for a variety of reasons. This "kind of" sounds biblical since we do believe our spirits live forever, even after death.

---

[55] 2 Corinthians 5:8, Luke 23:43

[56] Luke 16

However, the Bible is *very* clear about what happens to our spirits when we die. When my earthly life is finished, I have the promise that my spirit (the real me) will immediately be in the presence of Jesus, in the heavenly home He has prepared for me *forever*. I don't have to worry about haunting the earth with my unfinished business!

But what about those who are not believers? Could they be punished by being made to roam the earth as a ghost? As good as this plot may seem for a scary ghost story, God's Word tells us exactly what happens. The spirits of those who reject the love of God by refusing to believe Jesus go immediately to a place called Hell. One of the parables of Jesus shows us that spirits in this place have no contact with this world.[57] In fact, Jesus says there is a barrier that prevents unbelieving spirits from ever coming back to earth or communicating with those on it.

Is the Holy Spirit a ghost?

Very often in languages, certain words may stop being used or have their meanings change over time. Sometimes, people in a particular region will begin using a word differently. In English and some related languages, the words "spirit," "ghost," and "soul" are all used to mean the non-physical consciousness that lives in a body. "Ghost" has now wrongly come to mean this

[57] Luke 16.

eerie part of a person that hangs around after death working mischief or trying to find peace.

In early Bible translation, such as the King James version, "ghost" was used to speak of the 3rd Person of the Trinity—the *Holy Spirit*. The Holy Spirit (or Holy Ghost) isn't the soul of a dead being. He is just as much God as God the Son (the 2nd Person) and God the Father (the 1st Person) and has eternally been in a loving relationship with them. The Spirit has personality, emotions, will, and all the attributes of God. He is a *person*.

Even though we tend to give the Spirit less attention than the Father and Son, He is in all ways equal with them. In Scripture, the Spirit is perhaps less noticeable because He works more "in the background" of believers' lives. The Spirit actually *indwells* or "lives in" the believer (1 Corinthians 3:16). In addition, He does many other things for the believer…

- Teaches and reminds (John 14:26).
- Gives knowledge and wisdom (1 Corinthians 2:10-11).
- Reveals truth (John 16:13).
- Helps our weaknesses (Romans 8:26-27).
- Gives spiritual gifts (1 Corinthians 12:7-11).

Far from being an eerie ghostly presence that comes and goes, the Holy Spirit is always near and connected with our spirits, even when we don't recognize it. The Spirit is our constant, faithful helper in making us more like Jesus.

ABOUT JESUS…

Do we know the man Jesus actually existed?

The question is usually asked this way: "Do we know anything about Jesus other than in the Bible?" This is often called the *historical Jesus*.

There are numerous references to the man Jesus in historical documents from early historians Josephus and Tacitus. Interestingly, many facts about Jesus come from His enemies and critics whose writings obviously center on a real, historical person.

We should be careful, however, that we don't get the idea that the Bible is not trustworthy in telling us about Jesus (or anything else it tells us.) In another section we see evidence that the Bible is a very reliable account of Jesus's life and teachings.

What is Jesus's real name?

In a way, I have several names. I was born into the *McWilliams* family. My parents decided to give me the first name *John*. Sometimes, my parents called me *Son* and my close friends call me *Johnny*. Some names are more like titles that refer to something I do like *Teacher*.

Jesus has always been God (the second Person of the Trinity), thus we could refer to Him as *God* or *Lord*. In Jesus' time, names tended to describe a person in some way. Long before Jesus was born as a man, Isaiah said one of His names would be *Immanuel* which means "God with us."

At the beginning of the New Testament, an angel told Mary to name her child *Jesus*. This is the English pronunciation of the name *Joshua*, but His Hebrew family and friends would have called Him *Yeshua*. (In a similar way, other languages might pronounce *John* as *Juan*, *Jean*, *Johannes*, or *Ian*.)

As Jesus began His ministry, many called Him *Rabbi* (*Teacher*). Eventually, some of His followers realized that He was *Messiah*, the deliverer prophesied in the Old Testament. The title *Christ* (*Chosen* or *Anointed One*) was often added to His name. The term *Christ Jesus* or *Jesus Christ* would be like *President Washington*.

Because Jesus is the central figure in all of history and fills so many roles, Scripture uses many names and titles to describe him. Just to name a few…

Wonderful Counselor
King of Kings
Redeemer
Lamb of God
Prince of Peace
Alpha and Omega

How privileged we believers are to know Him as *Savior*, *Friend*, and *Brother*!

Why did Jesus have to die?

Jesus did many good deeds during His earthly life. He healed people and raised the dead. He taught principles that changed the whole world for the better. Two thousand years later, mankind is still reaping the benefits of the values preached by this Jewish carpenter.

But Scripture leaves no doubt about Jesus's primary mission on earth—to redeem sinful humans by sacrificing His life. His purpose was to die so that believers might live eternally!

In the Garden of Gethsemane, the night before His crucifixion, Jesus prayed to God the Father. He asked that if His mission could be accomplished in any other way, let that happen. The Holy Spirit answered Jesus's question. The only way to pay for the sins of the world was for Him to die as a sacrifice.

Our human minds have trouble understanding this aspect of reality—the fact that our sins can only be paid for by death. As eternal creatures, the price for our sinfulness would be to suffer an on-going death for eternity. The animal sacrifices of the Old Testament were only symbols pointing to what Jesus would one day do. In some way that is difficult to fathom, the death of a perfect, sinless man (Jesus) could be substituted for our deaths.

Jesus's death was not a tragic accident! He said "I lay my life down… No one takes it from me" (John 10:17-18). I am unspeakably thankful that Jesus obediently and lovingly suffered and died for my sin!

Was Jesus half man and half God?

In our earthly bodies with earthly fallen brains, we have limited understanding. I look forward to the day when my new heavenly body will finally begin its journey of eternal learning. Imagine, each day discovering more of God's unlimited universe. How many times will I say, "Oh, so that's the way that works!"

My earthly mind can't comprehend the Trinity—three Persons, yet one God. Nor can I understand how Jesus could be God and man. Jesus was completely, 100% human just like you and me. He experienced hunger, pain, joy, sadness, love, and even temptations. The difference was, He had no sin nature.

However, Jesus was also 100% God! In our math, this may seem a contradiction, but not in God's. The Trinity remained the Trinity while the 2nd Person, Jesus, walked the earth in human form. As a human, He did all the things that every human did (except sinning). He ate, breathed, got tired, and probably even skinned His knees. Jesus had human needs and desires (without sinning). He experienced happiness, sadness, love, wonder, anger, and frustration.

But what about the God-nature (*divinity*) of Jesus? In a way we don't understand, Jesus was able to "set aside" or not use some of His Godly abilities (see next section). Jesus had to grow up and learn things just like you and me! Scripture doesn't tell us how this worked or how much Jesus knew about certain "heavenly" things while in His earthly body. Whatever the case, Jesus set an example for us for living a life that is righteous and dependent on God the Father.

Did Jesus still know everything while He was a man?

Interestingly, Scripture tells us that the young man Jesus grew in size and *wisdom*.[58] If He was 100% God, didn't He already know everything? Wasn't He all-wise, being God? In some way, it seems that Jesus limited His own privilege to use His *divine* attributes.[59]

Jesus could have saved Himself from many situations (even His death) had He wished. He never stopped being all-powerful, yet He usually chose *not* to use His divine powers. There are times He seems to allow His omniscience in some cases. Jesus saw Nathanael under a fig tree even though far away.[60] He also knew the past actions of the Samaritan woman at the well.[61] Of course, when in accordance with the

---

[58] Luke 2:52

[59] This is called his *kenosis* or "self-emptying."

[60] John 1:48

[61] John 4

Father's will, Jesus could work miracles and call upon His divine nature.

Did Jesus ever say that He was God?

There have always been people who want to lower Jesus's status to merely a gifted human. They claim "Of course Jesus was a great teacher or prophet. He obviously was very 'tuned-in' to God, but He certainly *wasn't* God in human form, nor did He ever say He was God."

Although the writers of the New Testament all recognized Jesus as God, it's true that Scripture never records Jesus saying the exact phrase: *I am God…* But as you probably have learned, there are many ways to say something clearly without actually saying it.

First, Jesus was worshipped as God and was called God by others and He never corrected them. The Bible tells of several angel encounters in which a person falls down and begins worshipping an angel. Angels always stop the people and say something like, "Wait, hang on! I'm just an angel. Don't worship me." Jesus had opportunities to do this, yet He accepted worship as God. He also said, "He who has seen me has seen the Father." (John 14:9).

Jesus made the unusual statement that He existed before Abraham—2000 years before.[62] He claimed to be equal with the Father.[63] Jesus claimed the ability to

[62] John 8:58

[63] John 5:17-18

forgive sins which the Bible clearly teaches only God can do[64]

Perhaps Jesus's most obvious claim to be God is in His blatant use of God's name when referring to himself. In the book of John, Jesus uses the "Yahweh" name of God several times…

> I AM the way, the truth, and the light.
> I AM the good shepherd.
> I AM the vine.
> I AM the bread of life.
> I AM the light of the world.
> I AM the resurrection and the life.
> I AM the door.

These sayings lose their full meaning in translation. When Jesus used the "I AM" (Yahweh) name of God as the subject of His sentence, the references were quite clear to His enemies. He was claiming to be God! They grabbed up stones to kill him. When Jesus asked them why, they replied…

> It is not for a good work that we are going to stone you but for blasphemy, because you, being a man, make yourself God. (John 10:33)

There's no doubt that Jesus not only did the works of God, He communicated the fact throughout His ministry that he was indeed *God.*

---

[64] Mark 2:5–7; Isaiah 43:25

What does "Messiah" mean?

The Old Testament prophets predicted that one day, God would send the Jewish nation a special leader. This person, called the *Messiah*, would be the perfect king of Israel. He would bring justice, prosperity, and triumph over their enemies.

As with many prophecies, it was difficult for the Jews to understand the full nature of this future Messiah. Many thought the Messiah would be a great military leader, like King David. They understood that this "chosen one" would be a gift from God who would bring peace to Israel and the world.

What most failed to see was that *Jesus* was this Messiah. He would indeed bring peace to the earth and rule the world with justice, but it wouldn't be the way most pictured it. They didn't see that the Messiah's (Jesus's) first coming to earth would be to die for our sins. Not until His second coming to earth would Jesus finally create His peaceful and righteous kingdom.

How do we know Jesus really rose from the dead?

Did Columbus set foot on North America in 1492? Was President Lincoln assassinated while watching a play? Did Washington really chop down a cherry tree?

That's one of the problems with history. Unless we were there to see it, we may not believe it. We may hear from people who were there, or we may read reports written by people who were there. Either way—seeing is believing, or more accurately, not seeing might be not believing.

Most of the time we apply different levels of "trust" when we study historic events. When a lot of people or writings agree on something, we tend to believe it. If there is only one story about an event or if the storyteller is not believable, we usually find it harder to believe. The point is that with past events, we have ways of determining how reasonable an account might be.

Likely, the resurrection of Jesus is one of the most hotly debated historic events, and for good reason. If a human truly rose from the dead that would be the ultimate miracle! And the Bible is very clear on this—if Jesus *didn't* rise from the dead, how can we believe anything else the Bible says?

So, what do we know about Jesus's resurrection? What apologetic clues do we find in Scripture that show the biblical account is reasonable? Apologists have noted many different evidences, but I'll summarize just a couple[65]…

The people who lived at the time of Jesus's resurrection believed it. When the earliest New Testament books were written, many of the witnesses to the resurrection were still alive. Remember, hundreds of people had seen Jesus after His resurrection. If the story was just made up by the apostles, surely the public would have objected, "No way!" But this didn't happen. These

---

[65] For a deeper study, see *Evidence that Demands a Verdict* by Josh McDowell.

witnesses had no problem with what the New Testament said because *they had seen it*.

The leaders' responses. The Roman and Jewish leaders certainly didn't like the idea of Jesus rising from the dead. That would have meant they were wrong about everything. If the apostles had faked the resurrection, surely someone could have found Jesus's body or exposed the conspiracy. They tried their best, but no one could disprove the resurrection.

ABOUT THE CHURCH...

Is there one church or many churches?

The word translated "church" in the English Bible literally means "a gathering of people" (it never means a *building* like the way we use it). When the Bible uses the word, it may mean one of two things.

It could refer to simply a local group of believers. When Paul spoke of the "church at Rome," he meant the group of Christians who lived in the city of Rome. (Today, if I say "Missionary Grove Baptist Church" most people think of the building at a certain place, but it's actually the *people* who meet at that building.)

The New Testament mentions many of these *local* churches such as the church in Jerusalem, or the Laodicean church. A local church could be a few people meeting in someone's living room or thousands meeting in a huge cathedral. The Bible also speaks of "The Church." The meaning of *church* here is *the entire group of believers in Jesus from all over the world*. Every true believer is included in this church which is often called the *Bride of Christ*. Scripture tells us that this Bride will have a special relationship with Jesus (the Groom) throughout eternity.

Why are there so many different local churches?

But if all churches are part of one larger body, why can I drive down main street and see so many *different* Christian churches? I see Baptist, Methodist, Catholic, Presbyterian, Lutheran, Pentecostal, and about 5000 others! We call these various Christian groups *denominations*. A denomination is simply a church or group of churches that are different in some way from other denominations.

From the very first churches right after Jesus's ascension back into Heaven, there have been disagreements. Don't forget, churches are made of believers, but believers are humans. Humans have sin natures (even saved humans). We have different views about things. We make mistakes. We do selfish things. We get our feelings hurt. We hurt other people's feelings.

Someone said it right: "The church is a bunch of imperfect *saved* people who are trying to take the good news to a world of imperfect *unsaved* people." God would be pleased if every believer in every church was perfect like Jesus, but let's face it—that probably won't happen on this fallen planet. And make no mistake… God is constantly working to grow believers to be like Jesus, but it's a process. While the process continues, God patiently deals with us imperfect church members.

Some denominations began when a group of believers decided they would rather do things differently. For example, several people in a church might decide that they prefer to sing songs that are more modern than the old hymns. They then start their own church where they can sing what they want. This may not be a bad thing since it's possible to worship God with many types of music.

Sadly, some churches split into new churches because of fights and bad feelings among the people. This obviously doesn't display the love of God in a way that pleases him, but it happens often. I know a church that split from a larger group because the larger group had stopped doing some things that the Bible clearly said were correct. In this case, the new group could get back to biblical truth, although there were still hard feelings and anger.

The Bible allows us the freedom to have *preferences* in such things as music, preaching style, building decorations, whether to dress fancy or plain, how to spend finances, and many other details. We can worship and serve God with much diversity and creativity.

However, a line is crossed when God's Word is compromised. Over the years, some denominations have started over disagreements on important Bible doctrines or attributes of God.

When it comes to major truths in Scripture, God would not reveal two different truths that oppose each other. When two denominations disagree over an important biblical truth, one (or both) of them is wrong!

Society today likes to think that biblical truths are relative—that what is true for one person may not be true for another, as long as everyone is sincere in their belief. However, the Bible teaches that God is the standard by which we view truth. The truths in His Word remain true regardless of what a person or group of people think.

Also, when it comes to biblical truths, some are more critical than others. These are called *essential* and *non-essential* truths. It's not that some truths we're not so sure about, but rather some are essential for a person to be saved. For example, to be a true believer in Jesus, one would have to believe that he has the power to forgive our sins (essential truth). However, good believers may disagree on what a certain prophecy means or how to take communion (non-essential truths).

Although I'm free to differ in preferences (non-essential truths), the church I join should certainly teach and believe what the Bible says about essential truths. If I am wise, I will choose to attend a church that has a correct view of all the essential truths of God's Word. This doesn't mean that my church and its members will always be perfect, but that they are teaching the truth of God's Word and are trying to obey it.

Should I obey Christian leaders?

God invented governments with leaders and followers as a logical way for humans to live. In churches, He gave pastors and others to lead the church. In most cases, God speaks to church leaders who make clear the message and provide leadership. As a rule, we should expect Jesus to lead His Church through His leaders. We should pray for our church leaders and support them so that they can hear God and lead correctly.

Unfortunately, there are times in which some leaders may not obey God completely. Church members must be very careful in situations such as this. It would be very un-Christ-like to scream and rebel every time we disagreed with a leader.

If a Christian leader is clearly in opposition to an essential truth in Scripture, something must be done. Most Christians believe that we are not expected to follow a leader who is willfully disobeying Scripture or who is leading us into sin.

What about all the hypocrites in the church?

Churches are made of imperfect, sinful people who have been mercifully forgiven by Jesus's sacrifice! Just like schools, governments, and every other organization, there will be hypocrites, liars, and all types of sinners.

Hopefully, church members will be in the process of *sanctification* (becoming more like Jesus), but there is no guarantee of this. My responsibility as a church member is to make sure *I* am becoming more like Jesus. I should also help (in a positive, loving way) other members who may be struggling with sins. It's good to be as patient with our spiritual brothers and sisters as God has been with us.

Can I be a Christian and not attend church?

Members of the early New Testament church would have likely laughed at this question, but it is one asked by many people today. The Apostles would certainly wonder why a Christian wouldn't *want* to be involved in a church!

I've heard people say, "I can worship God best when I'm alone on a mountaintop" or "I can watch church on TV and sing to myself." This is true to some extent. Some of my most intimate moments with God have been while I'm alone with just Him. But it misses the point of why I need to be in a church.

If for no other reason, I should be an active participant in church because Jesus established it and called it *His church*. Also, the Bible tells us plainly that we should participate in church regularly (Hebrews 10:25). But there are many other reasons why church is an essential part of the believer's life. Meeting with other Christians regularly allows us to…

- Share each other's troubles and joys. It's always good to have a shoulder to cry on or someone to share my joy.
- Pray for each other. The best way to know what to pray for is to pray with others.
- Encourage each other. I need encouragement a lot, and fellow believers are always a rich source!
- Take care of each other's needs. By gathering with others, I can find out about

the needs of others and take care of them more effectively.

- Learn from each other. Sometimes God may give someone a special understanding that can help me.
- Worship God. Usually, worshipping God with other believers is even more fulfilling than worshipping alone.
- Be accountable to other Christians. Sometimes I have weird ideas that other believers can call to my attention and help me with.
- Fulfill the Great Commission. The *Great Commission* is what we call Jesus's command to "go to the whole world spreading the good news and teaching God's Word" (Matthew 28:19). This can only be done through believers working together!

Just as humans weren't meant to live apart from others, Christians weren't meant to act completely alone. There are times when private prayer, Bible study, and meditation are appropriate. However, believers should actively, and regularly, seek out the fellowship of other believers in Jesus's church.

It's also important to remember that church isn't just about what you *get* but what you can *give*. The church is like a body with many different parts. We all have different skills and talents. Furthermore, the Holy Spirit equips different people in the church to fill different roles or functions. Some of these mentioned in the Bible are gifts of giving, helping, wisdom, and teaching. If I fail to participate in a local church, I miss the opportunity to use my gifts and talents to help others and to glorify God.

Is it bad to believe Christianity is right and other religions are wrong?

There are many religions in the world besides Christianity. Some of them do great and kind things for people. In fact, many would agree with some of the truths in the Bible. There are a lot of people who are not Christians who do very, very good things!

God's Word, however, is very clear about one thing—salvation (forgiveness of sin, heaven, eternal life) is *only* through Jesus. In John 14:6, Jesus says, "I am the way, the truth, and the life. No one can come to the Father except through me."

The big difference between Christianity and all other religions is that all others teach that humans must please God by trying to do good things and not do bad things. God's Word tells us that we please God by believing and trusting Jesus.[66]

In our free country, we believe and respect that everyone has the right to believe whatever they wish. A person is completely free to have and express belief in any religion (or no religion.) We should certainly be *tolerant* of the beliefs of others, however, this doesn't

[66] After which, the Holy Spirit empowers us to *do* good things.

mean we must *believe* views that oppose the Bible are equal with biblical views. It's okay to disagree!

Scripture makes it clear that believers should stand for the truths given by God through His Word. We can respect and tolerate other's rights to differ, but still stand firm on biblical truths. This is especially important in our present culture which tries to shame believers into compromise.

The example is often used of a person in a burning building. That person may strongly believe that any door will lead to safety, but that doesn't work. Simply believing a door will save them is of no use. And if I know the only door that would save them, I'm obligated to tell them *even if they don't believe.*

Although a person's beliefs about salvation are eternally important, we must never be arrogant and mean when discussing the gospel with nonbelievers. Jesus set the example of love and kindness in dealing with those who did not yet follow Him. Our witness should be one that draws people to *want* to know and believe what we know about God's truth.

ABOUT SCIENCE...

Does God like science?

It surprises many people to learn that science was born from a biblical view. Other deities such as the Roman and Greek gods seemed to exist in a fantasy world with no solid physical laws. The God of the Bible, however, is orderly, dependable, and knowable. Early scientists who believed in this God could assume a universe that was *understandable* and *testable*. Just what science demands.

Johannes Kepler, the "father of astronomy," said his work was merely thinking God's thoughts after him. The Apostle Paul gives us one of the clearest connections between science and the Christian's experience...

> Ever since the creation of the world, His invisible attributes, namely, His eternal power and divine nature, have been clearly perceived in the things that have been made. (Romans 1:20)

Studying "what has been made" is a good definition of the true scientific process. In this verse, Paul says that there is enough evidence given about God through nature to make someone "without excuse" for not recognizing him. The book of Psalms also notes how the universe speaks to us about God...

> The heavens declare the glory of God, and the sky above tells of His handiwork. Every day it speaks to us, and every night it reveals knowledge. (Psalm 19:1-2)

Obviously, nature isn't a substitute for the gospel message, and the study of science in itself does not lead one directly to Jesus. However, Paul does imply that this clear evidence for an intelligent, mindful Creator should encourage unbelievers to search further. *Real* science glorifies God!

Since we have science, do we need God?

Imagine a person who grew up on a desert island with no contact with the rest of the world. Finally, he is rescued and taken to civilization. One day he finds a phone ringing. When he picked it up a voice came from it.

"Magic!" he cried.

"No," someone explained. "It's just an electronic device that changes radio waves into sound."

"Magic!" the man exclaimed again. "Magic must be causing the waves that the device picks up!"

"No," came a further explanation. "Another device far away is changing sound into waves and modulating the electromagnetic field."

"Magic!" the man cried again. "An electromagnetic field magically exists that can carry a signal!"

See what's happening? *Unknowns* were being revealed to the man one at a time. He's beginning to fill in the blanks in his knowledge with real physical actions.

In the 1800s, Christian scientists used the phrase *God-of-the-gaps* to try to correct the "lazy" thinkers among them. They were concerned that instead of using good science and logic, some people handled the gaps in our knowledge (unknown facts) by claiming, "It's a miracle from God!"

For example, when it was found that genes were the cause of inherited traits someone wondered, "Where do genes come from?" Another scientist suggested, "…From God! He put genes in us by a miracle!" It was later learned that our genes come from our parents at conception. There was no miracle, so that gap was closed. Then the big question is: *Will science eventually close all the gaps in our knowledge, meaning there is no need for God?*

No scientific discovery has disproven God, the Bible, or the Christian faith (and according to Romans 1, it never will). Yes, science will continue to reveal more and more about God's creation. We'll find out many more of the mysteries hidden in God's complex yet orderly universe. In a way, the fact that the universe works so well *without* constant, miraculous intervention is evidence that shows God's great creativity and wisdom.

But scientists are finding that all the gaps can't be closed. Science involves our senses examining the physical world. Science is really good at discovering the "whats" and "hows," but *totally unable* to uncover the "whys." The *why*-gap will always be beyond our physical senses and devices.

Physicists have theorized the universe back into the original singularity that "banged" into what we now see.

The *cause* of the bang, however, and the *reason for the cause* will ever elude science. Naturalistic scientists and atheists ignore logic problems and preach that science will eventually fill even the why-gap, but the physical limitations of science make this impossible. God will always be in that gap.

Is the Creation story in Genesis a real event?

In other sections of this book, we've examined the reasonableness of God and the Bible. Let's look at the creation just as the Bible does…

…in the beginning, God created…[67]

Scripture doesn't try to explain God. It simply states the fact of His existence and that He created.

As a Christian and a science teacher, I've dealt with this topic extensively. The evidence ranges from the simple observation of the orderliness of nature to discerning the complex origin of information in a molecule of DNA. Chapter 1 of Romans reminds us that there is so much obvious evidence for a Creator in nature (*things that have been made*), that all who refuse to believe are "without excuse…"

[67] Genesis 1:1. The opening verse of God's Word.

> For His invisible attributes, namely, His eternal power and divine nature, have been clearly perceived, ever since the creation of the world, in the things that have been made. So they are without excuse. For although they knew God, they did not honor Him as God or give thanks to him, but they became futile in their thinking, and their foolish hearts were darkened (Romans 1:20-21).

Note that the issue of nonbelief isn't due to a lack of evidence or even the misinterpretation of the evidence. The sad indictment is pronounced on those who *refuse to acknowledge* the Creator despite *knowing the evidence.* And the judgment has consequences in the here-and-now: *Their thinking became futile and their foolish hearts were darkened.*

The creation is too often portrayed as a death match between science and faith. In the 17th century, astronomer Johannes Kepler was one of many past scientists who had no issue with a universe of miraculous origin. Despite popular opinion, many contemporary scientists also see no discrepancy between science and Scripture.

And realistically, the *who* of creation is the easy part for Christians. It's the *how* that raises questions. Four primary views are common among scientists and others who consider origins. There are numerous subcategories, nuances, and overlaps, but we'll keep it simple…

1. Young Earth Creationism accepts the literal interpretation of events in Genesis. The days of creation were six, twenty-four-hour days. Earth's age is roughly 10,000-*ish* years. There was also a worldwide flood that brought about many features we observe on the earth's surface.

2. Old Earth Creationism asserts that the days in Genesis are *figurative* or *symbolic* references to long periods of time (billions of years). God created slowly, perhaps intermittently, all that we observe today, on earth and in the cosmos. Living things, including humans, were supernaturally created at appropriate times and experienced death for millions of years before the fall of Adam.

3. Evolutionary Creationism (theistic evolution) is basically the same as old earth creationism except that proponents acknowledge God used the process of slow evolution to bring life forms from ancient to modern. Little or no supernatural intervention was needed except perhaps in the very beginning.

4. Naturalism (Darwinian evolution) assumes only the physical universe. No intelligent, personal creator was needed, only random evolutionary processes. This is presumed to take long time spans to bring us to the present.

I appreciate the hard work of so many Bible-believing scientists who sift through piles of data from biology, geology, cosmology, and other fields related to origins. Like everyone else, I have my own view of creation events, but I've heard compelling arguments for the beliefs listed above (and several others).[68] There are still many questions to answer regarding *how* God created, and I would hope a healthy dialog will eventually resolve some of these.

It's one thing, however, to base views on legitimate data, yet quite another to disregard or eliminate particular alternatives simply because of their ties to supernatural intervention. I have a great deal of respect for scientists who might disagree with my take on origins because they have data that seem to support their conclusions. My problem is with Christian scientists who profess the supernatural as one of the bases of Christian doctrine, then reject it arbitrarily in practical applications to real events in the physical realm.

For example, the most flagrantly supernatural creation scenario is a literal six-day event, about 6000 years ago, in which God brings from nothingness the entire functioning universe, with strata and stars appearing to be of great age. Whether this is exactly true or not, the point is that often opinions rest on the degree of supernatural intervention with which one is

---

[68] My personal view of origins would be considered *young earth*. I realize there are data that seem to indicate a universe of extremely old age. I also see evidence that seems to contradict this, thus I've yet to find a good scientific reason for concluding one or the other. Because of this, my belief derives more from theology than from science. In my opinion, young earth creationism is the only alternative that addresses the sin/death issue. According to Scripture (New and Old Testaments), death entered the universe by Adam's sin. There have been many attempts to circumvent this allegorically or etymologically, but the results are less than satisfying. And, I have absolutely no problem with God's supernatural intervention in any way he desires. I suppose I'll remain in the young earth camp until I find a good theological explanation for death without sin or a Savior with no need to save us.

comfortable: "If we are uncomfortable with the supernatural appearance of age, let's discard that and add a few million years. If the miraculous arrival of millions of fully formed species is a problem, let's throw in slow evolution." Again, *God can do a big miracle as easily as a little one*. Beliefs should not be based on the *least supernatural* explanation.

What is *intelligent design*

For centuries we have pondered "Why is there something rather than nothing?" and "I think, therefore, I am." Science is somewhat limited in exploring these ideas, yet the created world undoubtedly affects our perceptions of them. These notions do lead scientists to ask two related questions: "Why is there *THIS something*, rather than nothing?" and "Why am I able to think about *this something*?"

These questions are especially troubling to those who refuse to believe in the Creator God. Seriously, why is the universe the way it is? There is no apparent rule within it that says it *had to be* this way. I can imagine countless ways it *could have been*. What if gravity was a little stronger? What if atoms had four primary particles instead of three? What if matter never condensed into planets and galaxies? In fact, why did there have to be any recognizable order at all? And that leads to the even more perplexing question "Why are we here as conscious beings able to ponder this order?"

Did you ever consider the complexity of a symphony orchestra? Imagine the collective hours of practice that prepared the mouths and fingers of the players. But don't stop there. Skilled players would be nothing without highly structured compositions to read and interpret. But keep going! Players and composers would be useless unless skilled instrument makers followed precise, orderly plans for producing violins, flutes, and horns.

Need I say more? Of course! There sits an audience with ears able to convert sound energy into electrical signals. And don't even get me started on the brains that can take that conglomeration of complex nerve impulses and enjoy a concert! Our whole universe is filled with not just complexity, but layer upon layer of complexity.

While *naturalism* (the belief that only the natural universe exists, with no God) struggles to explain the source of this order and structure in the universe, those who believe in a purposeful Creator have no problem. This is especially true if one accepts the Christian doctrine of the Creator God as being personal, eternal, loving, and unlimited in every attribute.

This *teleological* (the appearance of purpose and design) argument for God's existence has been discussed throughout history. We also call this *intelligent design*. In the 17th century, William Paley used the example of finding a watch along a pathway. Would we assume the watch was the result of chance events? Did all the individual pieces of the watch just happen to all come together? No, it obviously would indicate an intelligent, purposeful "watchmaker." In the same way, Paley reasoned, we look at the orderly world around us and assume a Creator.

The more we learn about the intricate workings of cells, biochemistry, astrophysics, and almost every other branch of science, the more evidence of complexity and purposefulness we tend to find. What Darwin and other scientists believed were simple cell functions are now known to be way more complex. And keep in mind, the only alternative to purposeful design is that random, blind chance is responsible for all that we see!

What about evolution?

But what about evolution? Is there evidence for it? It seems that many textbooks, museums, and TV science shows just assume that evolution happened and that we must be idiots for not believing it.

Many non-scientists choose to avoid this topic, thinking it takes a degree in biology to understand it. Yes, there is complicated material to interest the expert biologist, but the basic idea of biological evolution (usually called *Darwinian evolution*) is fairly simple.

In its simplest form Darwinian evolution says this: "All life that we now observe has come about due to small, random, mindless changes over long periods of time."

In other words, you are here now because of accidental chemical reactions that changed chemicals into cells, then to more complex animals, and finally to *us* all by blind chance. So, even a nonexpert, typical person could ask: "Does that sound reasonable?"

We could explore this idea in depth, and indeed many have. [69] For our purposes, though, the Romans 1 principle works quite well. Does our world around us *seem* to be the result of random, chaotic, purposeless changes?

---

[69] There are many excellent resources that explain and give evidence for intelligent design. A good starting place is www.discovery.org.

No. As we discussed earlier, the universe seems to be orderly, purposeful, and created. Could these "signs" of intelligent design be a mistake? Could the universe look purposeful and not really be? Paul didn't think so, and neither do a growing number of honest scientists today. I appreciate the fact that God has made the universe complicated enough to intrigue the experts yet simple enough to reveal Himself to everyone.

Digging Deeper Michael Behe, a leading intelligent design proponent, describes even some complicated systems which he describes as *irreducibly complex*. He uses a mousetrap as an example. There are seven parts that compose the traditional trap (wooden base, spring, trigger, etc.). If any of these parts were missing, it would cease to be a functional mousetrap, and according to Darwinian evolution, when a system loses function it will go extinct. Yet how could a mousetrap system ever evolve if it needed all seven parts at once to be a functioning mousetrap? What are the chances that all seven parts would have randomly come together *at the same time in the same place*?

Behe notes that biology is full of examples of this irreducible complexity. Even Darwin had problems with this concept in trying to explain how the human eye could have evolved with its many critical parts. What good would an eye be if it were lacking even one of these parts? And unless it was a functioning, beneficial eye, it would not have remained in the population.

How old is the earth?

Christians have different views about the age of the earth (and the universe in general). Two major views are common.

The *old-earth* view agrees with evolutionists that the universe is very, very old—around 10,000,000,000 (that's ten billion) years or so. "Old-earthers" interpret the rock layers in the earth and other data as showing this great age. Those who believe in evolution naturally require long ages, since evolution is assumed to be a gradual process that could not happen without extreme long time periods.

The *young-earth* view takes a literal view of the book of Genesis in the Bible. "Young-earthers" believe the creation account in Genesis should be read simply and straightforwardly—God used *six real, 24-hour days* to create the universe. That would mean the earth is roughly 10,000 years old.

This is a *huge* difference! There's no way to compromise these two ages and meet in the middle! Then who is right?

Remember, some beliefs about Scripture are *essential* and some are *non-essential*. Most Christians place these differences of opinion in the non-essential category. This certainly doesn't mean they are not important—just that we can disagree and still be followers of Jesus.

So once again, who is right? As a scientist, I can see evidence that points to both views. However, I tend to be a young-earther because of scriptural reasons…

- A simple, literal reading of Genesis seems to be speaking of real, 24-hour days.[70] (Old-earthers say these verses are simply poetic or figurative, and "days" could mean "eras." Thus each "day" might be a billion years.)
- If Adam's sin brought death to the universe, then old-earthers must explain how death happened for billions of years *before* Adam sinned (after the seven days of creation). That would mean that death would have been happening as long as living animals had existed. (Old-earthers would say that was millions of years before humans came along.) God would have created a system in which animals died violently and then proclaimed, "It is good." This seems out-of-character for God as He is described in Scripture.
- The Bible teaches that supernatural (miraculous and *un*natural) things can happen as God wills. Old-earthers usually have problems with supernatural events, thus a motivation for favoring long time periods. But creating something out of nothing *is* supernatural no matter how long it took! Couldn't God create in seven days as easily as billions of years?[71]

---

[70] The word "yom" almost always means a simple day. Also, each day references "the evening and the morning were the __ day."

[71] This would also explain the *appearance* of age. Old-earthers point to things in the universe which appear to be very old. But couldn't God have created a universe that way? In fact, didn't He? One second after Adam was created, he was probably observing large trees that appeared to be decades old although they had been created only days before.

You will likely hear many variations of young-earth and old-earth views. The important thing is to understand *that* God created, not necessarily *how* He created.[72]

Were Adam and Eve real people?

The event often referred to as the *fall of man* seems to be little more than a fairy tale today, even in many churches. Adam and Eve are considered myths, if acknowledged at all. Could their sins really affect us today?

Scripture is clear about the reality of the first human couple, and for good reason. Adam's sin was the cause for the fallen world and my sin nature. "Sin came into the world through one man, and death because of that sin" (Romans 5:12).

Jesus Himself spoke of the real-life Adam and Eve in explaining the significance of marriage vows (Matthew 19). Like any good Jewish boy, Jesus knew the Old Testament very well. Never in His teachings was there even a hint that certain parts were mythical.

So, what's the deal with eating the forbidden fruit? Why was this event so important? Here are some facts that Scripture gives us…

---

[72] For more discussions about age-of-earth views, see *answersingenesis.org*, *discovery.org*, or *reasons.org*.

- Adam and Eve originally had a pure friendship with God.
- The couple was in a state of innocence at this time.
- God always desired a free, loving relationship with humans. To test that relationship, He gave only one restriction—not to eat from a particular tree.
- In a free, selfish choice, Adam and Eve decided to disobey God.
- That choice (sin) broke their relationship with the Creator.
- The result was a "messed up," sinful nature within, and a "messed up" universe in which they had to live.
- All that could come from these *fallen* parents were fallen descendants (us).

Many have attempted to make God out to be the "bad guy" for being so harsh. But this is simply because they don't understand the *badness* of sin or the *goodness* of God. (Our sin nature has trouble accepting the idea that we have a sin nature!)

The modern view of humans is that we are "good down deep," but our experiences can make us bad (selfish, cruel, greedy, unloving, etc.) However, Scripture is very clear about our true human nature: "I know that good itself doesn't live in me" (Romans 7:18). At times, some people may choose to be "less bad" than they could be, but we all have a natural tendency to choose "bad." (Only the Holy Spirit can give us the power to choose "good.")

Not only did Adam's sin cause humans to have a fallen nature, but the entire universe was affected. We live in a world in which decay is normal. Things die. Animals eat other animals. Pain rules!

Does this seem like a condition for which God would say "It is good?"[73] Couldn't an omnipotent and omniscient Creator do better? Of course, He could—and He did. An imaginary Adam leaves us wondering why things are the way they are.

It's hard to imagine an *un*fallen condition, isn't it? My fallen brain has experienced only a fallen world with rotting things, sick things, and messed up things.

I'm thankful that God in His mercy didn't let the Story end here. Before the curtain falls on this tragic scene, the Creator promised a "fix." A rescuer would come who would reverse the sin of Adam and "reset" our fallen nature and the fallen world.

Does God use evolution?

You have likely studied the theory of *evolution* in school. In simple form, it states that groups of simple living things may change into groups of more complex living things over long periods of time. The process of *natural selection* allows some genetic traits to remain while others are discarded.

The reason this theory has biblical implications is that some use it to say that God (or any creator) is not

[73] Genesis 1.

needed to explain the world we see. More specifically, humans could be the result of random, mindless genetic changes instead of the work of a purposeful Creator.

There are some Christians who believe that God might have used natural selection (evolution) to bring about the millions of different living things on earth.[74] They would have an old-earth view of history. Of course, God can do whatever he chooses. If He wanted to use evolution to cause all living things, He certainly could!

A better question, though, is "Did He use evolution?" This is another point over which good Christians may disagree. The Genesis account seems to describe a supernatural, miraculous creation, not a long, bloody evolutionary process. If God used evolution, then He would have ordained the violent death of trillions of animals (before Adam's sin brought death). This seems to go against the nature of the God of life.

Was Noah's ark real?

For most of us, the story of Noah and the flood is etched in our minds from storybooks and coloring pages. But "two-by-two, floating zoo, rainbows,"—isn't all this better suited for a bedtime story than for real history? Can we believe what the Bible says about Noah, the ark, and the flood?

When we read Genesis 6 in an ordinary, literal way, it tells us that…

---

[74] This is called *theistic evolution.*

- Noah was a real person.
- The whole world was terribly sinful except for Noah and his family.
- God's holiness wouldn't allow the situation to continue.
- God mercifully allowed Noah's family to escape His judgment.
- God instructed Noah to build a vessel to escape the coming flood.
- All the people on the earth were destroyed except for Noah's family.

Those who question the literal truth of the Bible attack the flood story on several levels. Here are some of the criticisms used by doubters…

The story was just an imaginary lesson about sin and judgment. Just as with Adam and Eve, the New Testament (including Jesus) spoke of a real flood event. Nothing about the story suggests that it was a myth.

A loving God would never destroy the world and all those people. This feeling is somewhat understandable since our sinful natures don't like to think about how bad sin really is. Some people don't want to admit that being *perfectly good,* God hates sin and must judge it in righteousness. God was merciful to Noah and his family by providing a way to live in a better world.

The ark part of the story involved too many impossible things… Could eight people build such a large vessel? Could samples of every species on earth fit into the vessel? How would you collect all those animals? Wouldn't some animals eat others? How could eight people feed and water that many animals for over a year?

When we use the word "impossible" we should ask, "Impossible for whom?" Are any of these impossible for God? Of course not! If we believe that God created the universe supernaturally, why would we doubt that he could manage it supernaturally? The issue for Bible doubters isn't so much a problem with believing the story as it is a problem with believing in a miracle-working God and whether His Word is trustworthy.[75]

The flood was just a small, local event in Noah's village. Doubters use this to dismiss the miraculous nature of the flood and ark. If the flood was only a small area, then the ark didn't need to hold pairs of *every* species on earth, and it wasn't a big deal. But Scripture claims it was a *very big deal*! The whole earth and all of the human race was affected.

There is no evidence for a worldwide flood. On the contrary, we live on a planet whose surface is 75% sedimentary rock (produced by rock particles settling out of water). Sedimentary rock typically contains fossils. These are the mineralized remains of living things which appear to have been buried quickly in these

---

[75] However, when we really look at the flood account, there were only 3 supernatural acts: 1) the flood waters, 2) the animals coming into the ark, and 3) the closing of the ark's door. Some of the other aspects *could* have been miraculous but didn't have to be. For example, eight people working about 70 years could have built the ark. And not every single species was on the ark (probably no fish, crabs, jellyfish, etc.) The ark was *huge*. Plenty of room for land animal species. For full analyses of the flood events, these sites provide extensive resources: creation.com, answersingenesis.org, icr.org, or arkencounter.com.

sediments. The surface layers of the earth contain billions and billions of dead organisms. We also see much evidence of massive amounts of water eroding and depositing rock material.

Although we use it as a children's story, the flood event is one of the ugliest in Scripture—not just the death of so many people and animals, but the sinfulness that led God to be sad that He had created humans. The flood account teaches us much about God's mercy, grace, and righteousness. We should never minimize its importance by considering any part of it a myth.[76]

Is there life on other planets?

In his *Space Trilogy*, C. S. Lewis imagines a solar system filled with *Hnau* (non-human space beings). According to the storyline, the parents of these races never fell in sin as did Adam and Eve. Death, sin, and evil are dealt with differently than on fallen *Thulcandra* (Earth). Hnau are also able to communicate with the angelic beings and have an unfallen relationship with God.

Lewis's fiction did bring up some interesting theological questions. Are humans the center of God's dealings? If there are extraterrestrials (ETs), do they sin? If so, does God offer them salvation from sin? Did God

[76] For full analyses of the flood events, these sites provide extensive resources: creation.com, answersingenesis.org, icr.org, or arkencounter.com.

become one of them and live among them? Or do they have stories about a Savior who died for them in a galaxy far, far away? Will we someday teach them about Jesus?

These questions might sound odd, but the existence of non-earthly, conscious beings (other than angels and demons) would call for some theological answers. Today, we hear a lot about ETs, but despite our guesses, Scripture doesn't give a lot of clues about aliens. The Bible seems to place humans at the center of God's creative attention. God's grace, mercy, and love seem to be uniquely poured out on humans…

> "It is not angels that God helps, but the children of Abraham" (Hebrews 2:16).

This passage is a comparison with angels, but the implication seems to apply to any possible beings.

I often hear the argument: "If Earth is the only planet with conscious beings, then why is the universe so enormous?" This question doesn't consider God's revealed nature. Our Creator's resources are unlimited. He often goes above and beyond "merely adequate" just to show his glory and his love for his creatures. Flowers grow in fields where no one sees them. Amazing fish are doing amazing things miles below the ocean's surface in total darkness. Besides, it's no more difficult for God to make a universe than a flower!

So, are there ETs out there (besides angels)? *We just don't know…*

Personally, the adventurer in me would like to meet some aliens out there somewhere. Who knows—in the vastness of Eternity someday, will God choose to populate other galaxies with other beings? I can only imagine. Whatever the case, we can rest assured that any beings we might encounter, now or later, will be God's creation.

ABOUT THE BIBLE...

Are parts of the Bible just stories copied from other religions?

Suppose a group of people witnessed the assassination of JFK—different people, same event. That night, one of the observers was interviewed for a news article, and the account was published the next day. Then suppose fifty years later, a reporter doing a "historical" article interviews another of the witnesses and creates a fresh documentary. Someone now compares the two documents and exclaims "Copycat! The piece published later is obviously copied from the original!"

This mistake is very common among Bible critics who aren't aware of history or who choose to ignore it. We know that there are many ancient stories (older than Genesis) which include the first two people on earth who sin and are punished by their gods. Some of them include a garden or a snake, and they clearly mirror the biblical account. The same is true of the flood story. Sometimes, this is confusing to Christians who are taught that the Bible writers "borrowed" from other mythical stories.

The fact is, at one time, there was only one culture. When God divided humankind into many different cultures, each one would have still carried the same stories about their history. They would all remember stories about Eden, the fall, a serpent, angels, sin, a flood, and great-great-great grandparents who built a big boat.

Over time it wouldn't be surprising to find the different stories changed or purposely embellished to fit the new culture. Centuries later, when God inspired Moses to write the true versions of the stories, other older stories would naturally have some similarities.

I'm glad we have all of these similar stories about biblical events. Rather than making me doubt the biblical version, I believe these *extrabiblical* stories, even with their differences, actually support the ones in Scripture.

What is a worldview?

Some of my earliest memories are of the backyard on East 3rd Street. It seemed like a huge place. When I followed my dog Timmy to the back fence, the little tile house looked miles away. That was my world, along with occasional trips to town, church, and grandparents.

There were many mysterious things in my world. I recall watching through the fence as large, noisy trucks chugged by carrying long sticks on the back. Toward the end of most days, I remember hearing a low, mournful sound in the distance. Mama would comfort me, "It's just the mill whistle."

I didn't know what that meant, but it was enough to know that she knew and wasn't afraid. I began to look forward to the sound because it meant that in a little while Daddy would come home. He would always hug my sister and me as we met him at the door. Daddy smelled like something I never smelled in the backyard. I figured it was just daddy smell. When I sat on his lap, I remember seeing little brown flakes all over his clothes. His pants had tiny holes with dark edges that mine didn't. My little brain pondered a lot of these mysteries.

I'm not sure about the details leading up to this particular event. One day my dad put me in the car, and we went to an unfamiliar place. It was noisy. Stick trucks were everywhere. Little brown flakes were blowing into the car window onto my pants. The smell in the air was my dad's smell, but much stronger.

Daddy pulled the car up next to a tall machine and said "Wait here. I'll be right back."

I watched as my daddy climbed a ladder to the top. He put on a strange hat and fiery sparks began raining down the side of the machine. In a minute, he crawled down and shook a man's hand. Suddenly, I heard the sound again. The mill whistle—except it was so loud! Then another loud sound… I watched as sticks like the ones on the trucks started rising one by one into the huge building.

Something incredible had happened. My daddy probably didn't notice. When we got back home, there was no change that my mama could have seen. Yet within my little brain, a coherent worldview was starting to form. All those random, mysterious puzzle pieces of my life were fitting together. For the first time, I was beginning to see my world as a "big picture." Things made sense…

When I saw the trucks the next day, I knew they were taking trees to the mill. The mill whistle? Not so mysterious. It comes from where my daddy works. When he came home, smelling of sawdust, I could touch the holes burned in his pants and ask, "Did you fix machines today?" I could carry on an intelligent conversation with him! Even more important, I had a framework for new information. When Mama said Daddy had to work late, I understood that a lot of machines must be broken. When I saw a tree being cut down on TV, I could predict that it would be put on a truck and be taken to a mill. The world started to make more and more sense.

My worldview has continued to develop for several decades now. Each new factoid of truth I learn is a piece of a jigsaw puzzle. I go merrily through life picking up a piece here and another piece there, placing them securely in my idea bag. Over the years, I've collected a lot of information. It's a mixture of data about philosophy, TV, theology, friends, science, society, ethics, history, and such.

I have enough information in my bag to live a successful life. However, there are different ways to handle the information. When a new need comes up, I could simply sort through the random pieces until I find the appropriate truth. In theory, this would work, and it's probably how many people understand their world.

But I can think of a better way… Let's take the pieces out of the idea bag and lay them out on a table. It would be great to have a puzzle box top with a picture, but let's say we don't. My grandmother taught me the strategy of connecting the edge pieces first then looking for same-color pieces. So, the puzzle is beginning to take shape. And I'm learning an important concept—the pieces "fit" in one way better than in others. In fact, with the not-so-good fits I have to mangle and distort a piece if it fits at all.

As I find more fits, I'm becoming quite pleased with my puzzle-assembling skills! But something much more important is happening. Now, if someone were to say, "That piece doesn't go there," I would quickly reply "No way, it has to! Look at the way it locks in place perfectly with the other pieces and how the pattern matches. How could it not be in the right place?"

I'm beginning to see ideas in a *context*, not just randomly. It isn't just the information of the pieces, it's also their connections to other pieces. After adding a few more pieces, suddenly I see it!… I know what the picture is! "It's the Mona Lisa!"

The bag of random pieces now makes sense. There's a *context*. I can see the "big picture." That piece with a nose—it has to go here. And that piece with an ear—there. I can even predict what a piece should look like: "The piece that's missing on the left side of Mona's face has to have an eye on it…"

And perhaps even more important, I know what *doesn't* belong. Suppose some cruel puzzle-packer had slipped in a few pieces from a another, totally different puzzle. No problem. I can easily see that those "strange" pieces would never fit the context of the Mona Lisa. A worldview is kind of like this.

What are some common worldviews?

A worldview will address many questions about reality, but some of the main ones are…

1. What am I? (Where did I come from? What is my purpose?)
2. What is my world? (How do I deal with others? What is right and wrong?)
3. What is my problem? (Why is there pain and suffering? How can I fix it? Why is there evil?)
4. What is my future? (Will this world end? What happens when I die?)

Haven't you asked these questions in some form? Everyone does. The difference comes with how we answer them and how we fit these "puzzle pieces" together.

A strong *Biblical Worldview*[77] is important for a Christian, especially in today's world. There are many other worldviews around us such as Naturalism, Secularism, and Mysticism.[78] These worldviews see the

---

[77] Also called a *Christian worldview*. I like to use the term *biblical* because some Christians choose not to accept some biblical ideas literally.

[78] Naturalism – Sees the world as only the physical. No God, devil, soul, Heaven, afterlife.

Secularism – Says that humans are the basis for all truth. If the majority think it's true—it is. (Also called Humanism.)

same world as everyone else but interpret their experiences differently.

For example, with the very serious issue of whether very elderly people should receive the very best healthcare, these might be the responses of different worldviews…

- Biblical Worldview – "Yes! All people are God's image-bearers. We must honor that in any person at any stage of life."

- Naturalist Worldview – "No, the elderly take resources from others. And there is no eternal purpose anyway. Why prolong their life?"

- Secular Worldview – "If the community or family can support them, or if they are still contributing to society, then okay."

- Mystic Worldview – "Whatever those involved decide is okay. If it seems right, it must be okay."

Unfortunately, many people (especially young people, and even young believers) don't have any solid worldview, or they have worldviews that are random mixtures of all of these. What a confusing world it seems to them! Lack of a biblical worldview is why we see so much confusion and disagreement on so many important issues.

Mysticism – Teaches that there is no real truth except what an individual believes. (Also, called New Age or Hinduism.)

How do I build a biblical worldview?

This is a *very* good question for young believers. It's possible for a believer to live life without a strong biblical worldview. There are so many competing ideas coming at us from friends, school, TV, and the Internet that it's sometimes difficult to keep our worldview truly biblical.

The start of a strong biblical worldview is *a good relationship with Jesus and a good grasp of the Bible*. (Duh!) This is another reason for good habits of spiritual discipline. God's Word is effective in teaching us how to view and interpret the world around us. (I won't have a biblical worldview without knowing and believing the Bible!)

We also have other resources to help us understand and apply scriptural truths to our experiences. Good Christian *apologetics* (discussed earlier) helps tie worldview concepts together. In case you haven't noticed, one purpose of this book is to help build a biblical worldview. Many of the sections deal with "puzzle pieces" that fit together and reveal the big picture of reality.

There are many other resources for anyone wishing to strengthen their biblical worldview. The important thing is to *make the effort to do it*. Make it part of your spiritual discipline to keep putting the pieces together!

How did we get the Bible?

The Bible is a collection of 66 different books combined into a single volume. Those 66 books can be divided into two larger sections—the *Old Testament* and the *New Testament*. As we've already discussed, the 39 books of the Old Testament were written over several centuries before the time of Jesus.

Some of the events in the early history of God's people were passed from one generation to another through spoken or *oral* stories. For example, it's likely that Moses wrote the book of Genesis many years after the events themselves. He had heard the accounts from his parents who heard from their parents, and so on. (But remember, God still inspired Moses to write the histories *exactly* as He wanted.)

Eventually, all the Old Testament *historical books* were written by Jewish people in their language Hebrew (and some Aramaic). The Jews called this collection the *Torah*. During Jesus's life and ministry, He read and studied the Torah just like any Jewish young man. When Jesus referred to a certain Scripture, it was from the Torah.

After Jesus's death and resurrection, the early Church that He established began to grow. In the first years, they would have used the Torah, but also the new teachings of Jesus. Jesus's Apostles (the disciples whom He personally taught) would travel between the local churches (small groups of Christians who had believed the gospel of Jesus) teaching the new Christians how the truths about Jesus were the *fulfillment* or *completed ideas* of the Old Testament. In other words, the Torah was the true Word of God, but Jesus's message was that He had completed the message that was started in the Torah.

Over the next decades, the Apostles and other Christian leaders began writing letters to the spreading churches, explaining the "gospel ("good news") of Jesus death and resurrection. They explained how Jesus's death had paid for sins and that no more sacrifices were needed. These writings were passed from church to church so that all believers could learn the full explanation of God's truth. Eventually, the 23 accepted letters were combined into what we now have as the New Testament. The Bible (Old and New Testaments) now contained the complete message that God wanted people to have.

Both testaments are valuable to believers. The Old Testament provides rich insights into how God the Father deals with humans and what He expects. In the New Testament, the words and teachings of Jesus, His Apostles, and other leaders provide instructions for our salvation and for living the Christian life. When reading the Bible, it's good to read some of both testaments regularly.

Did God write the Bible or did men?

The Bible tells us that it has been "breathed by God." We call this *inspiration*. Sometimes we say that an artist was *inspired* to do a masterpiece, or that a leader spoke *inspiring* words. Biblical inspiration, however, is more. We mean that God caused a person to write exactly the words that He intended.

Inspired does *not* mean that God turned the writers into robots, as if they were writing in a trance. Miraculously, those who wrote the various books of the Bible were guided by God's Spirit to write from *their own skills, knowledge, and personality*. God is sovereign and able to shape the writers' experiences so that every word was *still His Word exactly!*

How do I know the copy of the Scripture I'm reading is the same as the original?

Did you ever play the "telephone game?" The leader whispers a phrase into one person's ear. That person whispers it to the next, and so on and so on. By the time the message reaches the last person it usually is nothing like the original.

Christian apologists have done much research into the *transmission* of Scripture—how it got from the original *manuscripts* to our current translations. We assume God supernaturally inspired only the original message, known as the *autograph*. Eventually, though, that writing would have to be copied. Back in the day, writing was on papyrus or animal skin which wouldn't last forever. Also, multiple copies would be needed to go to different places.

Bible copiers are humans, whether today or 3000 years ago, and there is no reason to assume they are supernaturally inspired in their copying. We expect mistakes to be made in copying. And certainly, when a copy is translated into a different language, there is no absolute guarantee that all would be exactly like the autograph. Today, we have *zero* autographs of the Bible—only copies.

Then how sure can we be that our *manuscripts* (copies) are true to the original? Can I trust that my Bible is accurate? First of all, early scribes took their jobs very seriously. History shows that they maintained strict standards of checking and rechecking, even counting characters much as a computer does.

In addition, other people were writing scripture passages (especially the New Testament) from very early times. Even those who opposed God's Word recorded scriptures in their arguments. Their writings help to verify the accuracy of manuscripts!

In the telephone game, we assume that the closer we are to the "front" of the line (the original whisperer) the less changed the message will be. With the same logic, we assume that the earlier the manuscript, the fewer the changes. This may not always be true, but it's a good starting assumption. We have manuscripts for most of the New Testament that were written within decades of the autographs.

As for the accuracy of the Old Testament, we were not sure until the 1940s. Around that time, a boy found a group of scrolls hidden in a cave near the Dead Sea. These Dead Sea Scrolls excited studiers of Bible manuscripts. The scrolls were written about 200 years before Jesus came to earth, much earlier than the copies we already had.

Amazingly (to those who doubted Old Testament accuracy), these manuscripts were almost identical to the more recent ones. We learned that over hundreds of years, the copies had hardly changed at all. The only changes were very small and didn't affect any major ideas. This gave good evidence that our present copies are quite accurate.

DIGGING DEEPER – The small differences we find among the manuscripts are typically just differences in numbers (such as the number of soldiers in a battle) or different spellings due to language changes. There are cases in which it appears scribes may have inserted their own "comments" into the text without noting them as additions. We also know that some manuscripts were purposely altered so that the true words didn't "offend" so much (obviously not a good thing). None of the questionable passages influence the "main and plain things" in the Bible.

And fortunately, we have numerous manuscripts to compare. If there is disagreement over which manuscript is the most reliable, you Bible probably has footnotes that say, "this verse is not found in some manuscripts" or "this phrase says ____ in some manuscripts."

The bottom line—we have very good evidence that the Bible we have has changed little since the autograph.

Who decided which books should be in the Bible?

I have a lot of books besides the Bible in my library. Many are by Christian authors who teach me much about God and His truth. However, none of these are divinely inspired as are the books of the Bible. They contain useful and reliable teachings about the Bible and Christian life, but they don't offer new truth not already in God's Word. So, how do we know the right books made it into the Bible we use?

The collection of inspired books in the Bible, called the *canon* of Scripture, was assembled over a period of time. Old Testament books were in use during Jesus's lifetime. This Torah had been collected over many centuries from the writings of Moses, the prophets, and others. Jesus quoted often from the Torah and never pointed out any errors. He even said that not a single letter of it would ever disappear. We assume that with Jesus's "stamp of approval," the Old Testament is just the way it should be.

The *canonizing* of the New Testament was a bit different. As the early churches were spreading, Jesus's apostles were teaching His truths in many. Most Christians considered their teaching to be inspired since Jesus had commissioned them personally to spread His Word.

When Saul of Tarsus became Paul the Apostle, his teachings were also seen as *authoritative,* or inspired by the Spirit. Most of the New Testament is composed of the Gospels (written by Matthew, Mark, Luke, and John) and letters written by apostles and other church leaders.

Despite what some Bible critics claim, there was little disagreement about which writings should be considered inspired, and thus, eventually included in the New Testament canon. Churches were already using the Gospels and letters before anyone "officially" pronounced them as inspired. Early Christians accepted them because the truths they contained worked! The teachings spoke with authority and agreed perfectly with what the apostles had taught.

As the church grew, other teachers had begun spreading other writings. Some claimed that these works should be considered inspired as well. Others disagreed. Eventually, there were meetings to agree on exactly which books should be in the canon. There was little question about the books in our present Bible, but many of the newer writings were not accepted as divinely inspired.

Some of the writings that were not canonized as our Bible books, are still considered inspired by some religious groups. These are often called *apocryphal* books. The Bible we now have is a proven book that has shown itself to be accurate, coherent, and useful for many centuries. Some apocryphal writings may be useful or interesting, but that doesn't mean they are inspired or without errors.[79]

If God was able to supernaturally inspire the writing of certain books, I believe He was certainly able to make

---

[79] For example, I would hope this book is useful and accurate. But I can't claim that I was inspired by God in the same way that biblical writers were. And as hard as I might try, I doubt that any of my writings are without error!

sure the Bible we have is just as He intended. We can assume that the original copies of each Bible book were perfect and approved by God.

Is the Bible *all* true?

When I got my pet hamster, Margaret, I didn't know much about hamsters, so I also got a book—*Everything You Need to Know About Keeping Your Hamster Happy and Healthy*. That book kept Margaret happy and healthy for a long time.

Whether the Bible is all true is an extremely important question, since the Bible is the way we know about God, salvation, living a Christian life, and reality in general. It's the only instruction book we have on staying spiritually healthy.

As already discussed, we expect God's message to us to be just that—*God's message to us*. But there are some who question whether all of the Bible is really God's Word. Here are some questions people ask…

Is every story and teaching in the Bible true? Some people like to "pick and choose" the parts of Scripture that are true. They say that some sections are God's Word, but others may be just people's ideas. If this were true, how would we know which parts to believe and which parts not to believe? What if my hamster book had some instructions that were just guesses inserted by the printer and not really the ideas of the expert? (Poor Margaret!)

Is every word, phrase, and punctuation mark in the Bible exactly the way God wants it? This may sound like an odd question but it's important. In other words, was the writer just trying to say what he *kind of* thought God wanted to say, or is it *exactly* what God wanted to say? What if my hamster book said, "Feed your pet three times a day," but the word "day" was changed to "year?" (Poor Margaret!)

Does the Bible contain all we need to know? Obviously, it's also good to know how to read, write, feed your hamster, and a zillion other things *not* in the Bible. But the Bible *is* all God wants us to know right now about him, salvation, and Christian living. We say that God's Word is *sufficient* in spiritual things. Books that discuss and explain Bible concepts are helpful, but we don't need additional spiritual ideas that are not already presented in Scripture. What if my hamster book didn't mention that hamsters need water? (Poor Margaret!)

Digging Deeper I believe the Bible is *inerrant* which means that the original manuscripts were completely the way God intended, down to the exact wording and punctuation. Jesus made the point that every letter and grammar mark in the Old Testament was true.[80] Also, Paul made a big deal out of whether a single word in the Old Testament was singular rather than plural.[81] Furthermore, 2 Tim 3:16 assures us…

---

[80] Matthew 5:18

[81] Galatians 3:16 (Abraham's *seed*, not *seeds*.)

All Scripture is breathed by God and useful for teaching, correcting, and training us to be righteous…

Why is the Bible so hard to understand?

Maybe we should rephrase the question before we start… "*Is* the Bible hard to understand?"

Suppose your friend left you a note to tell you where to meet that afternoon. If you're really good friends, you know how each other thinks. The note would be clear and understandable. Why would your friend want to confuse you or hide the meaning of the note?

The Bible is God's message to His people. He *wants* us to know His message! Would He give us a message that was unclear or hidden in a riddle? On the contrary, we expect His Word to His friends to be understandable.[82]

However, what if a stranger found your friend's note? It's possible that it may not be understandable to someone who didn't know you or your friend. In the same way, those who are not believers often find God's Word difficult or mysterious. Of course, if someone is seriously seeking to understand the Bible, the Holy Spirit will lead them to the truth about Jesus and salvation, just as He has done for all believers.

---

[82] This is called the *perspicuity* of the Bible. It is a *perspicuous* (meant-to-be-understood) message.

But having said all of this, the Spirit didn't dump the entire knowledge of God's Word into my brain all at once. God desires a *relationship* with me, not just a knowledge download! He often reveals scriptural truths slowly and steadily through prayer and studying His word. All of the "main things" in the Bible are the "plain things." Yet I will spend a lifetime digging out and contemplating new ways of applying the truths that the Spirit reveals.

But what about all the disagreements about the Bible?

It is certainly true that even though the Bible was meant to be understood, some still make it confusing. Often, however, the disagreements are over less important things (truths not critical to understanding salvation or the nature of God).

The Bible is a very diverse collection of writings. It has parts that are history, poetry, and instructions. Different writers also had different ways of looking at things. Some people disagree about whether a passage should be taken *literally* or *figuratively*. A verse taken literally could have a very different meaning when taken figuratively.

If your friend's note said, "Let's go hang out in the park," would you expect to find her clinging to a rope in a tree or sitting on a bench waiting? The figurative meaning would probably make more sense than the literal (unless your friend is just strange). The point is, you understand the meaning because you understand your friend and the context of the note.

That's another reason it's important to study the Bible regularly. You get used to knowing how the writers think. One part often gives clues for understanding other parts. The "big picture" view of the Bible makes more sense than just looking at random verses.

Sadly, it's also true that some simply want the Bible to say things that it doesn't really say. Many people today who don't want to obey the truths in Scripture try to interpret literal passages as figurative. It's much easier to deny Bible truths when they're viewed as symbolic rather than straightforward, plain truth.

Remember, there are some figurative passages in Scripture, but they are usually obvious. A wise person once said something like, "If the plain sense of the Bible makes common sense, don't look for another sense or you'll have nonsense!"[83]

Digging Deeper The various books of the Bible were written in Hebrew, Greek, and a little Aramaic. If you've ever studied a second language, you know that you can't just translate word-for-word. Different languages have different word order and "figures of speech" (idioms). As mentioned, "hang out" in English wouldn't be translated word-for-word to another language. (What if other speakers took it literally!) We would translate it into one of their phrases that meant "spend time together."

[83] David L. Cooper.

This means that in order to understand some verses we may need to know about the customs, idioms, and language oddities of the writer. Fortunately, we have learned much about these early Bible writers. We have the information to interpret Scripture accurately. If you have a question about a particular passage, do some research about it. Check apologetic resources and your pastor or other reliable people who believe the Bible.

Which Bible translation should I use?

Remember, the Bible wasn't written in English, so we English speakers should take care to choose a translation that gets across the original message accurately. As discussed, we can't do word-for-word translations because languages don't "fit" the same syntax patterns. Every translation will be someone's decision about what they think is the best meaning.

So then, it's very important to choose a Bible translation that was done by people (hopefully a group of scholars rather than just a single person) who really understand the two languages involved, and the customs and culture of the writers, and who really believe God's Word is true.

Also, consider the *purpose* of the translation. Some translators may want to produce more of a "storybook" for teaching general ideas or for reading to children. These may be good, but not necessarily translations one would use for understanding major doctrines. Some translations are meant to lean more toward modern

English idioms, others stay closer to the original Greek or Hebrew.

If you are a serious Bible student, I would recommend reading from several different translations. You don't even have to buy the Bibles anymore. Search the Internet for just about any verse (like Google "John 3:16"), and you'll find many sites with parallel Bibles. These will show the passage you are studying in several different translations.

Try to find a good *lexicon* for the Old and New Testaments. These reference books are useful in explaining various words and their meanings in the context of the original language. Or better still, if you have the opportunity and the desire, you may want to learn the original Bible languages. It will take time and effort, but it's quite rewarding to read and understand a passage from a true manuscript!

Isn't the Bible just a rulebook full of "don't-do-this?"

When I was very young, my parents gave me many *don't*-rules…

Don't go to the street.
Don't hit your sister.
Don't touch the stove.
Don't eat that bug.

Were my parents being bossy and unfair? I might have thought that at the time, but looking at the list now, all their rules were to protect me or make my life better.

Also, it was much more practical and efficient at this time in my life to tell me what *not to do* rather than what *to do*. ("Don't eat bugs" was more practical than "Do eat carrots, do eat bread, do eat cereal, do eat corn, do eat cookies, and so on…")

My car has an owner's manual that gives me a lot of rules. "Change the oil… Don't drive if warning light comes on… Don't run engine in closed garage… Fasten your seat belt… Slow down on ice…" What a bossy car maker!

Well, not exactly. The car's maker knows the capabilities of my car (better than I do). Who could possibly know *me* better than my Creator? Psalm 119 assures me that He even knew me perfectly *before I was born*.

Now add to this the fact that my Creator loves me with an unbounded love. Why would I ever want to question his rules? Not a single "no" from God is based on selfishness or randomness. Every "no" implies a "yes" to something else that is even better than what I think I'm missing!

ABOUT OTHER THINGS...

Why did God want innocent animals to be sacrificed?

Many people criticize the sacrificial system in the Old Testament. They ask why a loving God would use such bloody, uncivilized acts—killing innocent animals to atone for human sins? Others claim that the Israelites just borrowed the grotesque idea of sacrifices from their pagan neighbors. Animal sacrifices seem so cruel and barbaric to us today. Guess what... They also seemed cruel and barbaric to people back in the day.

Yet that was God's purpose. Animal sacrifices in the Old Testament were symbols pointing to Jesus's sacrificial death in the future. God allowed His people to see the sheer ugliness and terrible price that sin brought. When a Jewish child witnessed the sacrifice, they likely were thinking "This is all because of sin! My sin! Sin must be terrible!"

God's Word makes it clear that animal sacrifices (or any other sacrifices we could make) could never pay for our sins.[84] Only Jesus's payment could atone for our sins. This included all the sins of humans past, present, and future.

Like so many spiritual concepts, we as humans fail to see the real nature of sin. God is good, righteous, and just. Had there been a better way we must trust that He would have chosen it! Those who consider the symbol of animal sacrifice to be cruel then refuse to acknowledge Jesus's extreme sacrifice have missed the point completely!

Why was God so mean in the Old Testament?

I've heard some Bible doubters say that there seems to be two Gods in Scripture. They claim that Jesus shows us a loving, friendly God in the New Testament, but that God in the Old Testament is grumpy and judgmental.

We know that one of God's attributes is His *immutability* (unchangingness), so He couldn't be different from one time to another. However, in revealing Himself to humans we often see different attributes expressed at different times.

The Old Testament does describe how God had to take some severe actions. He ordered the Israelites to go to war and destroy certain nations. He even destroyed

[84] Hebrews 10:4

most of humankind in a flood.[85] Remember, though, the Old Testament events *foreshadowed* (pointed forward to) Jesus. Many Old Testament accounts showed us the ugliness of sin as seen by a holy God. This led people to hope for a "fix" for sin and death.

In the New Testament, God reveals the fix. The "good news" is that He mercifully provided a sacrifice for our sin through Jesus. The Old Testament judgments make us aware of the deep need we have for a savior who can forgive sin. The love, mercy, and grace of God have been working throughout the history of humankind, not just in the new Testament!

Today, many people like to imagine two different Gods. They want to concentrate more on God's love and mercy than on his judgment and anger. However, we must remember that God doesn't change. He still hates sin—the same types of sin he hated in the Old Testament. We who love Him should avoid sin in all its forms, even though we know there is forgiveness through Jesus.

Why did God choose the Israelites to be His special people?

God is a loving, personal being, who desires relationships with His creations. From the beginning

[85] Even among these harsh cases in the Old Testament, God still showed Himself to be extremely loving and merciful in many instances.

chapters of Genesis, God was seeking friendships with those willing. He walked with Adam and Eve in the garden before they sinned. Afterwards, He told them to multiply and fill the earth with people.

But by Noah's time, almost all the people of the earth had turned their backs on God. Through humankind's rebellion and destruction, God saved Noah and his family as a fresh start. A few centuries later, humans were rebelling again at Babel. God was forced to stop their plans, spreading them over the earth and in a sense disowning them.

Yet God didn't give up. From an obscure tribe in the city of Ur, He chose a man as the father of a new people group. He spoke to the shepherd, Abram, telling him His plan to build a nation from his descendants. This "chosen people," through no merit of their own, would receive God's mercy and grace, and become an example to the rest of humankind as to what God is like. They would receive, record, and spread His truths.

Most importantly, from this people, God promised that a special person would come. This *Messiah* would somehow fix all of the failures of humans and restore a relationship with God. The Messiah (Jesus) did come through the Jewish nation just as God promised, although many of them at that time didn't believe He was the one.

Does it matter which music I worship with?

A character in a Shakespeare play noted how strange it is that a vibrating string could move the human heart. Basically, he was marveling at how musical sounds can affect human emotions in so many ways. Music can bring us happiness, sadness, calmness, excitement, encouragement, and just about any other emotion.

I don't understand the psychology involved, but I know that music is a powerful thing. According to Scripture, humans didn't invent music. Angels were singing God's praises long before mankind. Interestingly, Lucifer (who became Satan) was originally the leader of the heavenly symphony. The Bible speaks of many types of music from funeral dirges to joyful choruses. It's no wonder then, that music has long been used in human praise and worship. God is pleased with music. He invented it!

Like other good things God created, music can obviously be used in bad ways. For now, though, let's just think about the music we sing and play at church. Traditionally, most church services include what is called *praise and worship* music (P&W).

These terms are often interchangeable, but usually *praise* is associated with *thankfulness*, and *worship* with *adoration*. The P&W music during my church's services allows me to *adore* God for who He is and *thank* Him for what He has done for me.

Sadly, however, music has become an arguing point in some churches. Does God care about the type of P&W music we use? Well, "yes" and "no"…

God made us all with different musical preferences. I'm sure you know there are hundreds of musical genres from which to choose—pop, rock, jazz, country, folk, rap, bluegrass, southern gospel, and many others Almost all of these "styles" have probably been used in some way as P&W music. Worshipping God in your preferred musical style is okay.[86]

The important thing is that it truly does glorify God. Music may uplift me and make me feel good, but does it accomplish God's objective in my life? I think there are some guidelines that might help in choosing the music we use for P&W…

- Does the music glorify God, or does it mainly just make me feel good? It's okay to feel good while worshipping, and good P&W music will do both. However, glorifying God is always what matters!
- Does most of my P&W music teach or emphasize biblical truth, or is it just repeated phrases? Simple choruses are okay, but they are like dessert. I can praise God best with music that nourishes me with solid biblical truth. Traditionally, hymns were based on Scripture passages and were useful ways to emphasize deeper spiritual concepts, *along with* praising and worshipping.

[86] Although I can think of some types of music that I can't imagine being worshipful or glorifying to God, simply because they have become associated with ungodly themes.

- Is the music *wrong* about some biblical truths? Unfortunately, there are songs that try to pass as good P&W but have some unbiblical ideas. If the lyrics of a song make me question truths that I know to be biblical, I might need to hold the lyrics up to Scripture and check with my pastor.
- After I participate in P&W music am I closer to God or just happy over the experience? P&W music might make me feel good, but the main result should be a closer friendship with God and a desire to obey His Word.

And certainly, don't make this list into a bunch of new "guilt" rules. Humans are complex beings. Sometimes during the music at my church, I appreciate the talent of a particular singer or player. Or I may think the melody of a certain song is really nice.

It's okay to enjoy P&W music on many different levels. God created the reality of sound, chords, harmony, lyrics, and every other good thing in the universe. We can enjoy the creation because we love the Creator!

ABOUT THE FUTURE…

What is Jesus's second coming?

Just before His ascension into heaven after the resurrection, Jesus promised His followers…

> I am going to prepare a place for you and I will come again and will take you, so that where I am you may be also. (John 14:3)

One of the clearest and most joyous truths in Scripture is the bodily, earthly return of Jesus back to this earth. The *first coming* of Jesus was His incarnation as a baby who lived thirty-three years in this world. He lived as a humble, suffering savior who meekly obeyed the Father and died shamefully on a cross.

But if He was truly the Messiah, what about the prophecies that portrayed the Messiah as a triumphant king and majestic ruler of all the earth? One of the reasons many Jews rejected Jesus was because He didn't fit these *messianic* prophecies. Jesus was hated by the world and died in dishonor, didn't he?

It was difficult for people back then to see that the prophecies spoke of two separate events. The New Testament, however, sheds more light on the *second coming* of Jesus.

God's intent is for believers to be about doing His work here on earth. Although we gain much hope from knowing that Jesus is coming to set up a righteous kingdom on earth (the first one ever!), we must not let our anticipation prevent us from spreading the gospel and living obedient, productive lives.

Perhaps God left parts of His Son's second coming shrouded in mystery to keep us watchful yet always busy doing what needs to be done. Because all the details aren't given in Scripture, there are disagreements among those who study the prophecies of the second coming.

Most of these are over the *when* and the *how* and not *whether* Jesus is returning. Generally, these are the main events centered around the second coming…

- Jesus descends from heaven, just as He left 2000 years ago—in His glorified, physical body.
- A judgment for unbelievers to finalize their unwillingness to be part of Jesus's kingdom.
- A judgment of believers to give them rewards for faithfulness.
- The establishment of a 1000-year, worldwide, righteous kingdom that will bring peace and prosperity to earth.
- After 1000 years, the heavens and earth are restored to their unfallen state and eternity in a perfect universe begins.

What is the Rapture?

There are some aspects of Jesus's second coming that seem a little confusing on the surface. One passage says all people will see Him when he arrives. Another has Jesus coming "secretly" and only a few will see. One passage says He will be "in the air," while another says He will stand on earth." Many who take Scripture literally see that these "inconsistencies" are quite easy to explain.

The Bible actually describes two *phases* of Jesus's second coming. He will certainly come to the earth to set up His real, earthly kingdom, and every person on earth will be aware of this. However, several passages speak of a mysterious, secret appearance of Jesus just before this…

> For Jesus Himself will come from heaven with a shout, the voice of an archangel, and the sound of the trumpet of God. Believers who have died will rise first. Then we believers who are alive will be caught up together with them into the clouds to meet Jesus in the air, so we will always be with Him (1 Thessalonians 4:16-17).

This event in which believers are "caught up together" is often called the *rapture*. The rapture will involve only believers (dead and alive). Jesus will appear "in the air" and only believers will see Him. Dead believers from all ages will be instantly resurrected with glorified physical bodies and immediately after, living believers' bodies will be transformed in glorified bodies…

> In the blink of an eye, at the last trumpet, the dead will be raised with eternal bodies, and our bodies will be changed (1 Corinthians 15:52).

Naturally, non-believers wouldn't believe that Jesus would actually return to earth one day. However, some in today's church seem to ignore the reality of the rapture and the second coming. We should expect doubters according to the apostle Peter. He tells us that they will say…

> Where is the promise of Jesus's coming? As long as we remember, all things are continuing as they have from long ago.

In other words, people will dismiss the idea of Jesus's return because it has been so long, and it hasn't happened yet. What a dangerous belief! Scripture tells us that God could be delaying Jesus's second coming in order to give sinners more time to repent.

There is also some disagreement about the timing of the rapture. Will it happen 7 years before the actual second coming or 3 ½ years before? Or will it occur just seconds before Jesus comes to set up His earthly kingdom? Although some believers disagree, the most literal reading of Scripture suggests the rapture will happen first, then the 7-year *Tribulation*, and then the second coming.

Whatever your belief about timing, the rapture is a joyful event for believers. God's Word calls it the "happy hope."

When will Jesus come back to earth?

Jesus very clearly warned that no one knows the "day and hour" of His bodily return to earth (except the Father).[87] On the other hand, He urged believers to watch for the signs of His coming. He provided several such signs that would mark the "season" of His coming. The message seems clear: *Don't try to set a date, but be aware of the approaching time...*

This is the biblical, healthy attitude that believers should maintain. The doctrine of Jesus's second coming should never cause obsession and bitter disputes.

What if I don't want Jesus to come back yet?

I knew a couple who took their two young children to Disney World. It was about a 300-mile trip, so Mom prepared an "activity box" with all kinds of puzzles, books, games, and such to keep the kids entertained. It was a big hit. The children loved it. As they finally

[87] Matthew 24:36

pulled into the park entrance Dad announced, “We’re here!”

The children whined in unison, “Noooo! Can’t we just stay here and finish the game?”

The children had no idea what this “Disney place” was like. Their parents had tried to explain the awesome rides, the characters, the shops… But the young children couldn’t imagine such wonders. The activity box was *here*—Disney World was *out there*.

It’s very normal to be anxious about the unknown, even if there’s every reason to believe it’s wonderful and unthreatening. As a young person, I loved Jesus, but I didn’t necessarily look forward to Him coming back and ending my earthly plans. I had dreams about the future—a family, career, and a long life!

If you don’t feel the return of Jesus is the “happy hope” the Bible describes, it’s okay. God understands. If your future life looks promising, it’s difficult to imagine a more promising life in God’s kingdom. But like the Disney World example (and infinitely better), there’s no comparison.

God loves His children. He would never reward us in eternity by taking away a *good* thing to replace it with a *less good* thing. Rejoice in the fact that as a believer, your next move (whether Jesus returns or you experience death) will be an “upgrade,” not a loss. Paul realized this truth…

> For me, to live is Jesus, and to die is even better. If I am to live in the flesh, that means I can keep working for God… It’s hard to say which I prefer! But my main desire is to depart and be

with Christ, for that is far better (Philippians 1:21-23).

What if I'm afraid to die?

If you fear death, welcome to the club! You're just like every other normal person who ever lived!

Death wasn't part of God's original design for any of His creations. And in fact, our souls (the real us) *will live forever*. Only your present physical body will one day die. (Unless, of course, you are a believer who is alive when Jesus returns!)

The Bible so clearly assures me that as a believer my death will simply be my passing to a new realm—one far better than this one in every way! Yet still, it's sort of an unknown to me. My friends once convinced me to ride a rollercoaster I had never ridden before. I had ridden others, but this one was new and unfamiliar. They had all ridden this one and assured me how much fun it was. *But I was still a little bit afraid...*

Jesus promised He was going away to prepare a wonderful home for me in heaven. He had been there before! He knew it was wonderful! I believe Jesus, and I know my future home will be great. *But I'm still a little bit afraid...*

It's okay! God understands my fears! As a believer, one day the real me will leave my earthly body and be placed into a new heavenly body.[88] It will *still be me*, but with no pain, fear, or imperfections.

We're also sad and a bit fearful when loved ones die. Scripture says that's okay, too. But God's Word also says it's a type of sadness "not like the unbelievers." We have the sure hope that if our loved ones are believers, they will immediately go to be with Jesus when they die. They're enjoying a face-to-face conversation with Him before you are! What a joy (even in the temporary sadness) that as believers we will all be together again someday. My faith looks forward to that day!

What will Heaven be like?

We hear about "heaven" so often…

"That cake is heavenly!"

"Good heavens!"

But when the Bibles speaks of Heaven, it's a *real* place. In fact, it's more real than this physical world in a sense. Heaven is the place where God is. It's His home and the place where Jesus said He would prepare a special place just for us. It's the place that will live forever.

As mentioned previously, any place with which we are unfamiliar is a bit scary. That's understandable. And it's why God gives us clues in His Word to let us know there's nothing to fear.

---

[88] The Apostle Paul says it will be like taking off an old coat and putting on a new one (2 Corinthians 5).

From another perspective, Heaven is that place that all of us long for deep inside. We all dream about wonderlands, Narnias, and somewhere over the rainbow. Some people say that's just wishful thinking. I believe we imagine those places because *we were made to live in a place like them*. Our hearts long for our future home!

So why doesn't the Bible tell us exactly what Heaven is like? One reason is that it's so good, there's nothing on earth to compare it to…

> What no eye has ever seen, no ear ever heard, and no heart ever imagined, this is what God has prepared for those who love Him (1 Corinthians 2:9).

My heart can imagine some pretty awesome things, yet heaven is even better! Try to think of things that our unlimited, loving, generous, omniscient, omnipotent Creator can come up with! Can we even begin to imagine what He will provide for us motivated by unlimited grace and love? It doesn't simply stagger my imagination—it's way beyond it!

I've heard people worry about Heaven, saying "I don't think I'll like sitting on a cloud playing a harp all day." Others say, "But won't Heaven be like a long, boring church service?"

What sad misconceptions of Heaven! The word "boredom" won't exist in Heaven. Besides being a place where some things don't exist (pain, tears, fear, evil), Heaven is a place of activity. Not only will we finally be face-to-face with our Creator forever, we'll do things with Him. Scripture tells us we will *reign* with Him.

There will be adventure, discovery, amazement, and accomplishment and it will get better and better! And you will still be *you*—not some ghostly, nameless whatever! You will know and love believers you knew and loved on earth, and even more! (Pardon the exclamation marks, but Heaven is an exclamation mark kind of place!!)

Some people believe we shouldn't think too much about Heaven because there's still too much work to do here on earth. I disagree. The more I think about Heaven, the more I want to "put my treasure" there. This isn't selfish greed. Scripture tells us to serve God here on earth so that your Heavenly treasure will increase. I don't know what that means exactly, but it makes me want to get busy and serve Jesus!

The truth of Heaven also makes me want others to be there with me. I want to tell as many people as possible about the good news of Jesus so that their eternal home will be Heaven, also.

Will my pet be in Heaven?

I've heard people say, "Why are you concerned about whether your pet will get to heaven when so many people need to get there?" Yes, of course people are more important than animals, but animals are pretty important to a lot of people!

The usual line is that people have eternal spirits and animals don't. Scripture does speak of human spirits, but it doesn't give many clues as to the mental nature of animals, although it does encourage kindness to all creatures. Does my cat have a soul or spirit or consciousness? Will some part of her live on after her body passes? The honest answer—we just don't know.

On the other hand, I know that God is overwhelmingly graceful, loving, and generous. Even though I don't know for sure, it certainly wouldn't surprise me to see my pets at the home Jesus prepared for me. I like to think my dog Oreo will be wagging her tail waiting patiently just inside Heaven's gates.

GLOSSARY

Angel – The role of messenger assigned by God to some of the heavenly beings. Sometimes it can apply to a human messenger, such as a pastor.

Apocrypha – Writings used by some groups such as Catholics that are not in our Bible (such as the Book of Maccabees, or 1st Enoch). There may be useful material in apocryphal books, but they are not considered inspired.

Apologetics – The study of how to offer evidence for the truths of the Bible.

Atonement – Paying a debt. Making things right. Specifically, Jesus's payment for our sins.

Demon – One of the angels who followed Lucifer in his rebellion against God. These *fallen angels* still follow Satan's (Lucifer's) orders.

Grace – God's choice to give us rewards we don't deserve. (Compare with "mercy.")

Essential truth – A fact or reality in God's Word that must be understood and accepted in order to become a child of God.

Hebrews – See Jews.

Incarnation – Jesus coming to earth as a man. The 2nd Person of the Trinity taking on a physical, human body.

Israelites – See Jews.

Jews – Also called Hebrews, Israelites, The Chosen People, or Israelis. This is the nation selected by God to convey His truths to the rest of the world.

Judeo-Christian – This term refers to the principles and worldview taught in the Bible. The Bible is from both a Jewish and more specifically Christian perspective. Orthodox Jews and Christians still hold many values in common.

Lucifer – One of the most beautiful and powerful heavenly beings ever created by God. At one time he led the other beings in praising God. But one day Lucifer decided to rebel and take over heaven. God cast him out of heaven, and he is now the devil or Satan.

Mercy – God's choice to not give us the punishment we deserve. (Compare with "grace.")

Michael – One of the chief angels (archangel) mentioned in Scripture.

New Testament – God's written word given to people after the resurrection of Jesus. In the Bible it's the 27 chapters from Matthew to Revelation.

Naturalism – The belief that only the natural world exists and that there is no supernatural. Thus, there would be no God, spirits, miracles, or afterlife.

Old Testament – God's written Word given to people before Jesus came to earth as a man. In the Bible it's the first 39 books from Genesis to Malachi.

Paradox – A situation that *seems* to be impossible or contradictory on the surface but has good reason to be true. For example, Jesus was 100% man and 100% God.

Redemption – To buy something or pay a price. Specifically, Jesus paid the price for our sins.

Resurrection – A dead physical body coming back to life. (Not simply resuscitation like doctors may do.) Specifically, Jesus living again after His death on the cross.

Salvation – Being saved from our sins and eternal death by Jesus's death on the cross.

Sanctification – Becoming more like Jesus. The process of a Christian growing spiritually day by day.

Saved – Salvation. Being rescued from our sins by Jesus.

Savior – One who *saves* others. This is a name given to Jesus since He saves us from sin and eternal death.

Trinity – The three-person nature of the one true God—Father, Son, and Holy Spirit. Sometimes called the *Godhead*. God is three Persons, yet one Essence.

Scriptures noted in the text (ESV)

Acts 5:3–4 - But Peter said, "Ananias, why has Satan filled your heart to lie to the Holy Spirit and to keep back for yourself part of the proceeds of the land? While it remained unsold, did it not remain your own? And after it was sold, was it not at your disposal? Why is it that you have contrived this deed in your heart? You have not lied to man but to God."

Acts 16:31 - And they said, "Believe in the Lord Jesus, and you will be saved, you and your household."

Corinthians (1st) 13:4-7 - Love is patient and kind; love does not envy or boast; it is not arrogant [5] or rude. It does not insist on its own way; it is not irritable or resentful;[b]
[6] it does not rejoice at wrongdoing, but rejoices with the truth. [7] Love bears all things, believes all things, hopes all things, endures all things.

Corinthians (2nd) 4:17 - For this light momentary affliction is preparing for us an eternal weight of glory beyond all comparison.

Daniel 4:35 - All the inhabitants of the earth are accounted as nothing, and He does according to His will among the host of heaven and among the inhabitants of the earth, and none can stay his hand or say to him, "What have you done?"

Deuteronomy 32:4 -The Rock, His work is perfect, for all His ways are justice. A God of faithfulness and without iniquity, just and upright is He.

Ephesians 2:8 - For by grace you have been saved through faith. And this is not your own doing; it is the gift of God.

Exodus 3:14 - God said to Moses, "I AM WHO I AM." And he said, "Say this to the people of Israel: 'I AM has sent me to you.'"

Exodus 34:6 - And he passed in front of Moses, proclaiming, "The LORD, the LORD, the compassionate and gracious God, slow to anger, abounding in love and faithfulness."

Genesis 3:15 - I will put enmity between you and the woman, and between your offspring and her offspring; he shall bruise your head, and you shall bruise his heel.

Hebrews 1:6 - Faith is the assurance of things hoped for, the conviction of things not seen.

Hebrews 12:1 - Therefore, since we are surrounded by so great a cloud of witnesses, let us also lay aside every weight, and sin which clings so closely, and let us run with endurance the race that is set before us

Hebrews 13:2 - Do not neglect to show hospitality to strangers, for thereby some have entertained angels unawares.

Hebrews 13:8 - Jesus Christ is the same yesterday and today and forever.

Isaiah 46:9-10 - Remember the former things of old, for I am God, and there is no other. I am God, and there is none like me, declaring the end from the beginning and from ancient times things not yet done, saying, "My counsel shall stand, and I will accomplish all my purpose."

James 4:2-3 - You desire and do not have, so you murder. You covet and cannot obtain, so you fight and quarrel. You do not have, because you do not ask. You ask and do not receive, because you ask wrongly, to spend it on your passions.

James 5:16 - Therefore, confess your sins to one another and pray for one another, that you may be healed. The prayer of a righteous person has great power as it is working.

Jeremiah 32:17 - Ah, Lord GOD! It is you who have made the heavens and the earth by your great power and by your outstretched arm! Nothing is too hard for you.

John (1st) 1:9 - If we confess our sins, he is faithful and just to forgive us our sins and to cleanse us from all unrighteousness.

John (1st) 4:7-8 - Beloved, let us love one another, for love is from God, and whoever loves has been born of God and knows God. Anyone who does not love does not know God, because God is love.

John (1st) 5:20 - And we know that the Son of God has come and has given us understanding, so that we may know him who is true; and we are in him who is true, in his Son Jesus Christ. He is the true God and eternal life.

John 3:16 - For God so loved the world, that he gave his only Son, that whoever believes in him should not perish but have eternal life.

John 3:19 - And this is the judgment: the light has come into the world, and people loved the darkness rather than the light because their works were evil.

John 10:28 - I give them eternal life, and they will never perish, and no one will snatch them out of my hand.

John 14:9 - Jesus said to him, "Have I been with you so long, and you still do not know me, Philip? Whoever has seen me has seen the Father.

John 16:13 - When the Spirit of truth comes, he will guide you into all the truth, for he will not speak on his own authority, but whatever he hears he will speak, and he will declare to you the things that are to come.

John 7:24 - Do not judge by appearances, but judge with right judgment.

Luke 2:52 - And Jesus increased in wisdom and in stature and in favor with God and man.

Luke 3:22 - And the Holy Spirit descended on him in bodily form, like a dove; and a voice came from heaven, "You are my beloved Son; with you I am well pleased."

Malachi 3:6 - For I the LORD do not change…

Matthew 7:13-14 - Enter by the narrow gate. For the gate is wide and the way is easy that leads to destruction, and those who enter by it are many. But the gate is narrow, and the way is hard that leads to life, and those who find it are few.

Matthew 7:21-23 - Not everyone who says to me, "Lord, Lord," will enter the kingdom of heaven, but the one who does the will of my Father who is in heaven. On that day many will say to me, "Lord, Lord, did we not prophesy in your name, and cast out demons in your name, and do many mighty works in your name?" And then will I declare to them, "I never knew you. depart from me, you workers of lawlessness."

Peter (1st) 1:3 - Blessed be the God and Father of our Lord Jesus Christ! According to His great mercy, He has caused us to be born again to a living hope through the resurrection of Jesus Christ from the dead.

Peter (1st) 2:2 - Like newborn infants, long for the pure spiritual milk, that by it you may grow up into salvation.

Philippians 1:2 - Grace to you and peace from God our Father and the Lord Jesus Christ.

Proverbs 3:5-6 - Trust in the LORD with all your heart, and do not lean on your own understanding. In all your ways acknowledge him, and he will make straight your paths.

Psalm 139:7 - Where shall I go from your Spirit? Or where shall I flee from your presence?

Psalm 34:8 - Oh, taste and see that the LORD is good!

Psalm 71:19 - Your righteousness, O God, reaches the high heavens…

Romans 1:20 - For his invisible attributes, namely, his eternal power and divine nature, have been clearly perceived, ever since the creation of the world,[a] in the things that have been made. So they are without excuse.

Romans 6:1-2 - What shall we say then? Are we to continue in sin that grace may abound? 2 By no means! How can we who died to sin still live in it?

Romans 8:18 - For I consider that the sufferings of this present time are not worth comparing with the glory that is to be revealed to us.

Romans 8:19-23 - For the creation waits with eager longing for the revealing of the sons of God. For the creation was subjected to futility, not willingly, but because of him who subjected it, in hope that the creation itself will be set free from its bondage to corruption and obtain the freedom of the glory of the children of God. For we know that the whole creation has been groaning together in the pains of childbirth until now. And not only the creation, but we ourselves, who have the first-fruits of the Spirit, groan inwardly as we wait eagerly for adoption as sons, the redemption of our bodies.

Romans 8:26 - Likewise the Spirit helps us in our weakness. For we do not know what to pray for as we ought, but the Spirit himself intercedes for us with groanings too deep for words.

Romans 8:28 - And we know that for those who love God all things work together for good,[h] for those who are called according to his purpose.

Romans 8:37-39 - No, in all these things we are more than conquerors through him who loved us. For I am sure that neither death nor life, nor angels nor rulers, nor things present nor things to come, nor powers, nor height nor depth, nor anything else in all creation, will be able to separate us from the love of God in Christ Jesus our Lord.

Romans 10:13 - For everyone who calls on the name of the Lord will be saved.

Romans 10:17 - So faith comes from hearing, and hearing through the word of Christ.

Samuel (1st) 2:2 - There is none holy like the LORD, for there is none besides you.

Timothy (2nd) 1:9 - [God] saved us and called us to a holy calling, not because of our works but because of his own purpose and grace, which he gave us in Christ Jesus before the ages began

Made in the USA
Coppell, TX
13 November 2021

65687777R00118